David McLellan was born in Hertford in 1940, and was educated at Merchant Taylors' School and St John's College, Oxford. He has been Visiting Professor at the State University of New York and Guest Fellow in Politics at the Indian Institute of Advanced Study, Simla, India. He is currently Reader in Political Theory at the University of Kent. He has lectured widely in North America and on the Continent of Europe and his publications (which have been translated into many languages) include *The Young Hegelians and Karl Marx* (1969), *Marx before Marxism* (1970), *Karl Marx: The Early Texts* (1971), *Marx's Grundrisse* (1971), *The Thought of Karl Marx* (1971) and *Karl Marx: His Life and Thought* (1973).

Modern Masters

Marx

David McLellan

Fontana/Collins

First published in Fontana 1975
Second Impression October 1975

Copyright © David McLellan 1975

Made and printed in Great Britain by
William Collins Sons & Co Ltd, Glasgow

Contents

1 Introduction

The inaccuracies in the obituary of Marx published in the London *Times* are an indication of how little he was known when he died. But in the century or so since his death, Marx's name – whether revered or reviled – has become known to all. Paradoxically, this widespread influence has not always aided the comprehension of what Marx had to say. In the sphere of politics this is understandable: as part of the ideological equipment of mass movements, Marx's writings have too often been reduced to ill-digested slogans. And their piecemeal publication has meant that only recently has a coherent picture been able to emerge. So it is not surprising that Marx still remains so misunderstood. It is simply not true, for example, that Marx ever described the historical process as a movement of thesis, antithesis and synthesis; or that his ideas were refuted by the Russian Revolution in that, according to him, a revolution could only come about in the most advanced industrial countries; or that he believed the standard of living of the working class would inevitably decline; or even – on a more personal level – that he lived in enforced poverty and died at his desk. Yet all these statements are widely believed.

These misapprehensions are all the more striking when the extent of Marx's influence is considered; no more than seventy years after his death one-third of the world lives under political systems claiming direct inspiration from Marx's ideas and his followers are a force to be reckoned with everywhere else in the other two-thirds. Intellectually, Marx's influence has been as great as it has been politically, and this influence is not only confined to the obvious subjects of politics, economics and history. There is scarcely a discipline to which scholars working from a 'Marxist' point of view have not brought insights. To take two rather surprising examples: in the field of literary criticism, the work of the Marxist George Lukács is gaining increasing attention; and one of the most influential schools of theology on the Continent stems from Ernst Bloch's interpretations of the young Marx. It is not only in sociology where development can largely be described as a dialogue with the ghost of Marx.

There are several reasons why Marx himself is so elusive. Marx was a thinker on the grand scale. In a world of increasing specialization, it becomes difficult to follow a thinker who not only mastered so many disciplines but also managed to integrate them. This broadness of his sweep was due to several factors: Marx was a cosmopolitan, rootless, Jewish emigré intellectual; he had moved rapidly from the idealist hyper-intellectual opposition movements in semi-feudal Germany, through the perfervid socialist sects of Paris, to mid-Victorian England – 'the demiurge of the bourgeois universe' as he called it; he received a classical education and was steeped in a philosophy which drew its inspiration from Antiquity in general and the aristocratic ideal of the Greek *polis* in particular. When tired of economics, Marx relaxed by reading Thucydides and the classical authors that were 'ever new'. He read all Aeschylus in the original every year. He was one of the last Renaissance men.

This cultural breadth inherited from Germany matched well with that general enthusiasm for system building and all-embracing theories of the Victorians. Marx was in a good position to observe Victorian capitalism: in 1851, two years after he arrived in London, there opened the Great Exhibition in which as he put it, 'the world bourgeoisie erects its pantheon in the new Rome where it proudly places on show the deities it has fabricated'. And 1867, the year in which Marx published Volume One of

Capital, marked the height of the liberal era. It was an age of manifold inventions, of swiftly increasing supplies of all sorts of goods and services, an era in which progress could be, and was, charted almost daily. There was also a greatly enlarged range of facts at the disposal of the researcher and a 'realism' made itself felt everywhere from the politics of Bismarck to the novels of Zola. After all, science was making spectacular advances and Comte had already given a name to the final and supposedly all-embracing science – sociology. This sense of progress and of realism was fully absorbed by Marx along with the confidence in the values of freedom, democracy and rationality that were common to all thinkers in that period of exceptional middle class stability.

But to say that Marx was a Victorian is not to deny that he has much to say to our more stormy times. Marx's method of analysis has survived even where its content is no longer of great interest. The broad question with which Marx tried to come to grips – the causes and destiny of the economic revolutions of his time – is with us still. Above all, the delicate dialectic between progress and catastrophe haunts the present generation as much as it did Marx:

At the same pace that mankind masters nature, man seems to become enslaved to other men or to his own infamy. Even the pure light of science seems unable to shine but on the dark background of ignorance. And our invention and progress seem to result in endowing material forces with intellectual life, and in stultifying human life into a material force.

Early Years

When Marx wrote in the *Communist Manifesto* that as the class struggle approached its decisive hour a section of enlightened bourgeois intellectuals would join the proletarian cause, he may well have had himself in mind. For he was born, in 1818, into a comfortable middle-class home in Trier, the commercial capital of the Moselle wine-growing district, the oldest city in Germany and one of the most beautiful. Two factors predisposed him to take a critical look at German society. Firstly, he came from a long line of rabbis on both sides of his family: his father, although intellectually a typical rationalist of the Enlightenment who knew his Voltaire and Lessing by heart, had only agreed to baptism as a Protestant on pain of losing his job as one of the most respected lawyers in Trier; his mother, whose horizons were bounded by the problems of her household, was strongly influenced by Jewish piety. Secondly, there was strong opposition in the Rhineland to its domination by semi-feudal Prussia. For the Rhineland was not only the most advanced area of Germany industrially, but had been annexed by Napoleon and much influenced by the principles of the French Revolution.

Having spent five rather undistinguished years in Trier High School, Marx went to the University of Bonn in 1835 at the age of seventeen. There he enrolled in the Faculty of Law, was strongly receptive to the romanticism dominant at Bonn and spent a lot of time, drinking, duelling and writing poetry dedicated to Jenny von Westphalen, to whom he had become engaged the same year. Jenny was the daughter of Baron von Westphalen, a city counsellor in Trier who had already interested Marx in romantic literature and Saint-Simonian politics before his departure for Bonn.

Marx's father considered that his eldest son was not living up to his high expectations at Bonn and sent him to the far larger and more serious-minded University of Berlin in 1836. Here Marx remained for the next four years. He wrote innumerable poems, a complex classification of legal concepts three hundred pages long, a comic novel, a tragic play, and a new basic system of metaphysics. With the astonishing capacity for rapid assimilation that distinguished him throughout his life, he filled notebook after notebook, moving from law towards philosophy, and finally abandoning Romanticism in favour of the Hegelianism then dominant in Berlin – an intellectual evolution that Marx described in a long and fascinating letter to his father. He summarized his newly acquired view: 'if the gods had before dwelt above the earth, they had now become its centre'. Very soon Marx abandoned his formal studies and began to prepare a doctoral thesis. He was spending a lot of his time in the company of the radical Young Hegelian intellectuals, led by Bruno Bauer, who were engaged in turning the destructive side of Hegel's dialectic against his system and moving from a critique of religion to one of politics. Marx's thesis had the rather obscure subject of the difference between the atomic theories of Democritus and Epicurus, but like most of the Young Hegelians he saw a parallel between post-Aristotelian and post-Hegelian philosophy.

The thesis completed, Marx had hoped to obtain a university teaching position through the good agencies of Bauer, but Bauer himself was dismissed for unorthodoxy in early 1842. More or less disowned by his mother (his father had died in 1838), Marx decided to try to make a career out of journalism. His reputation as a mordant critic was high among his Young Hegelian friends, one of whom described him as follows:

He combines the deepest philosophical seriousness with the most biting wit. Imagine Rousseau, Voltaire, Holbach, Lessing, Heine and Hegel fused into one person – I say fused, not juxtaposed – and you have Dr Marx.

In the spring of 1842 Marx began writing for the *Rheinische Zeitung*, an opposition daily backed by liberal Rhenish industrialists. He contributed articles on the freedom of the press, and religion in politics, and in October became editor. The paper's circulation increased by leaps and bounds, but increasing difficulties with the censorship authorities led to its suppression in March 1843.

Marx was not unhappy to be freed from his editorship: he was, as he put it, 'head over heels in love', and made immediate preparations for his marriage to Jenny – they had already been engaged for seven years. Instrumental in the suppression of the *Rheinische Zeitung* had been Marx's exposé of the miserable poverty suffered by the Moselle wine growers, a piece of work that led him, as Engels said later, 'from pure politics to economic relationships and so to socialism'. But first of all Marx felt the need to return to his study and come to terms with Hegel's political philosophy. This he did in the summer of 1843, staying at his mother-in-law's house in Kreuznach. He read Rousseau, Montesquieu and Machiavelli, as well as numerous historical works on the French Revolution. In the resulting unpublished manuscript, entitled 'Critique of Hegel's Philosophy of Right', Marx definitely rejected Hegel's idealistic justification of contemporary German politics.

Paris and Brussels

Marx decided to emigrate to Paris. For several months he had been discussing with one of his Young Hegelian friends, Arnold Ruge, the possibility of producing a Franco-German journal to unite German theorizing with the progressive

politics of the French; and Paris, the hothouse of innumerable socialist sects, made an ideal centre. Marx arrived
there in October 1843 and settled in the Latin Quarter,
sharing a house – as an experiment in community living –
with his co-editor and other German exiles. Marx's contributions to the *Deutsch-französische Jahrbücher* were
two articles, *On the Jewish Question* and an *Introduction*
to the manuscript on Hegel's political philosophy that he
hoped to publish later. But contact with workers' clubs and
the general political atmosphere of Paris made a rapid
impression on Marx whose growing communist tendencies
led to a break with Ruge. The *Deutsch-Französische Jahrbücher* failed to attract French collaboration or make itself
commercially viable and never got beyond its first issue.
But Marx continued his reading on the French Revolution
and began to turn his attention to the classical English
economists. Ruge found the pace altogether too fast:

> Marx reads an enormous amount; he works with
> uncommon intensity and has a critical talent that some-
> times degenerates into a wanton dialectic, but he finishes
> nothing, is always breaking off and plunging afresh into
> an endless sea of books.

As the summer wore on, Marx conceived of the plan of
writing a series of monographs dealing with law, morals,
politics and so on, and began to collect material for the
first one on political economy. These notes became known
as the 'Economic and Philosophical Manuscripts' or 'Paris
Manuscripts' and contained extracts from the English
economists, a description of humanistic communism as an
alternative to contemporary alienated society and a critique
of Hegelian philosophy. Marx passed a lot of time with
the poets Heine and Herwegh, fellow-exiles, and the
Russian anarchist Bakunin, and spent whole nights discussing the Hegelian dialectic with the leading French
socialist Proudhon.

In September a lifelong friendship and collaboration was

born when Frederick Engels met Marx in Paris. Engels was the son of a Rhenish cotton spinner whose firm had a branch in Manchester where Engels had been working. He brought Marx a practical acquaintance with the workings of capitalism, an ever-ready source of financial assistance, and the one firm friendship that Marx enjoyed throughout his life. Engels stayed two weeks in Paris, almost all the time talking to Marx. The two friends decided to collaborate on a book attacking Bauer and their former Young Hegelian colleagues. The polemic, ironically entitled *The Holy Family*, was scarcely finished when Marx was expelled from Paris for subversive journalism.

Marx settled for the next three years in Brussels where there was a considerable German emigré population and a comparatively free press. Before leaving Paris he had signed a contract for a book on economics and politics, and in the summer of 1845 he began to renew his studies of economics with a visit to England where Engels acted as guide. During the last three months of 1845 the two friends were engaged in writing *The German Ideology* which set out their newly acquired materialist conception of history and was designed to 'settle accounts with our erstwhile philosophical consciousness'.

While in London, Marx had met the leaders of the League of the Just, a semi-clandestine organization of emigré German artisans whose headquarters had originally been Paris. In Brussels Marx founded a network of communist correspondence committees to keep German, French and English socialists informed about each others' ideas and activities, and to try to introduce a minimum of theoretical unity into the nascent communist movement. In this context, two important disputes occurred during 1846. In the first Marx opposed in the Brussels Committee the views of Weitling, a journeyman tailor who advocated an imminent revolutionary insurrection. Marx's view was that 'the bourgeoisie must first come to the helm', and he prevailed. Secondly, Marx wrote the *Poverty of Philosophy* to oppose the eclectic socialism of Proudhon whom he had previously invited to represent Paris on the network. This is how Marx appeared to Annenkov, a Russian emigré who met him just as he was beginning to make an appearance in the German working-class movement:

Marx himself was the type of man who is made up of energy, will and unshakable conviction. He was most remarkable in his appearance. He had a shock of deep black hair and hairy hands and his coat was buttoned wrong; but he looked like a man with the right and power to demand respect, no matter how he appeared before you and no matter what he did. His movements were clumsy but confident and self-reliant, his ways defied the usual conventions in human relations, but they were dignified and somewhat disdainful; his sharp metallic voice was wonderfully adapted to the radical judgements that he passed on persons and things. He always spoke in imperative words that would brook no contradiction and were made all the sharper by the almost painful impression of the tone which ran through everything he said. This tone expressed the firm conviction of his mission to dominate men's minds and prescribe them their laws. Before me stood the embodiment of a democratic dictator such as one might imagine in a day dream.

By 1847 the League of the Just became conscious of the need for a firmer theoretical foundation for their activities and decided to approach Marx and Engels, who were eager to enter the working-class movement in which they placed such high hopes. During two long Congresses in London the ideas of Marx were accepted in principle by the League (renamed the Communist League), and Marx was commissioned to set them down in a *Manifesto*. This classic document was scarcely drafted when it was overtaken by the 1848 revolutions.

The Year of Revolutions

In France, the working-class National Guard turned against King Louis Philippe who abdicated to make way for a provisional government of liberal tendencies with a more radical socialist wing. This government invited Marx back to Paris. He accepted the invitation all the more readily as the Belgian government had just expelled him for contravening his undertaking not to engage in political journalism. On his arrival in a Paris still littered with the debris of recent barricades, Marx opposed the current idea of a German workers' legion to liberate Germany: their task, he said, was to assist the revolution in Paris. By March, however, the revolution had reached Berlin and King Frederick William IV had been compelled to grant an elected Prussian parliament, a free press and an Assembly to draw up a new Constitution. Marx immediately moved to Cologne and resumed his journalistic activities of five years before. The Communist League being more or less superfluous, Marx concentrated his energies during the following hectic year on the editorship of his new paper, the *Neue Rheinische Zeitung*.

In terms of circulation and impact the paper was a great success. It called itself an 'organ of democracy' and advocated the two points of 'a single, indivisible, democratic German republic, and war with Russia which would bring the restoration of Poland'. During its first few months the paper made virtually no reference to working-class politics and concentrated on working for the emancipation of the bourgeoisie – a point of view which necessarily led to friction between Marx and the more radical artisan association in Cologne. By the autumn, the watershed of the revolution had passed: reaction triumphed in France and Austria, but Marx still favoured an alliance with the more progressive elements of the bourgeoisie and refused to support separate working-class candidates for elections. His paper was encountering increasing difficulties with the authorities but it was not until April 1849, a month before the collapse of the revolutionary movement, that Marx changed his tactics and advocated separate working-class political action. But it was far too late: the last number of the *Neue Rheinische Zeitung*, printed in red, appeared on 18th May.

Marx returned once again to Paris, always optimistic: 'a colossal eruption of the revolutionary crater was never more imminent than now in Paris,' he wrote to Engels. But it was not to be. In July, the now familiar expulsion order arrived and in August he sailed for England to begin his long sleepless night of exile.

Exile in London

Marx's fourth child was born soon after his arrival in England. Funds allowed the family only a few months of the comfortable life they were used to living before eviction led them through a series of temporary lodgings to the three-room flat in Dean Street, Soho, where they stayed until 1856.

Marx was anticipating the outbreak of fresh revolutions in Europe and attempted to continue his journalistic activities by founding a monthly entitled *Neue-Rheinische Zeitung-Revue*. In it, Marx published a series of essays, later entitled *The Class Struggle in France*, in which he reconsidered the significance of the 1848 revolutions. He was also occupied by the activities of the Communist League whose reconstituted London branch he had joined immediately on arrival. At first, Marx attempted a *rapprochement* with the Blanquists, but the reading that he had begun in the British Museum soon convinced him that 'a new revolution is possible only in consequence of a new crisis'. This led to a split in the Communist League with those who thought his attitude too quiescent. Engels departed to work for his father's firm in Manchester and Marx soon retired from active politics. He belonged to no political organization for the next ten years.

The years in Dean Street were characterized by a constant lack of money. The fourth child, Guido, died in 1850 and another child the following year; but the worst blow to Marx was the death of his eldest son, aged eight, in 1856. Marx wrote to Engels: 'My wife is ill, little Jenny is ill, Lenchen [the maid] has a sort of nervous fever. I could not and cannot call the doctor as I have no money for medicine. For 8–10 days I have fed the family on bread and potatoes and it is still questionable whether I can get any together today.' Understandably, these domestic worries ground down Marx's naturally optimistic character: 'There is no greater stupidity,' he wrote to Engels, 'than for people of general aspirations to marry and so surrender themselves to the small miseries of domestic and private life.' It should be noted that Marx's income would have been quite adequate, had he known how to manage it carefully, but both he and Jenny had an extravagance (and generosity) that entailed continual financial crises. Marx was often to reflect that he, who wrote so much on capital, should have so little talent for managing it. The domestic situation was further complicated in 1851 by the birth of an illegitimate son to Helena Demuth, the German maid who had followed the family through all their peregrinations and was the only member of the household to have some domestic common sense. The father was Marx, but Engels (who had quite a reputation as a womaniser) agreed to accept paternity; the child was sent to foster-care, and the whole matter hushed up.

A small legacy in 1856 enabled the family to rent a house off Haverstock Hill, but the necessity of keeping up the appropriate appearances soon brought back the trips to the pawnshop. Marx wrote in typical vein to Lassalle in 1861:

> As far as my book is concerned, it will not be ready for two months. In order to avoid starvation during the last year I have had to do the most contemptible sorts of job and have often not been able to write a line of the stuff for months on end. In addition, it is characteristic of me that if I see something that I completed four weeks or so ago, I find it unsatisfactory and rework it completely.

In the same year, Marx informed Engels of the repercussions of this on their family life: 'My wife tells me every day that she wishes she were in the grave with the children and really I cannot hold it against her; for the humiliations, torments and fears that we have to endure are in fact indescribable.' It was not until 1864 that the death of his mother and a legacy from Wilmelm Wolff brought substantial relief. But as financial worries receded, Marx's health deteriorated: like Job he was plagued by boils from head to foot. He dosed himself with such extraordinary medicines as creosote, opium and arsenic, but the boils continued to debilitate him for years on end and he could only comfort himself by reflecting that the bourgeoisie would have good cause to remember his sufferings from 'this truly proletarian disease'. Nevertheless – like many men who appear intolerant in their professional capacities – Marx had a very warm home life: he loved playing with his children and the week regularly culminated with the Sunday picnic on Hampstead Heath accompanied by singing and recitations from Shakespeare.

Marx's only regular source of income in the 1850s (apart from Engels) was his articles for the *New York Tribune*, a radical paper with the largest circulation in America. These covered all aspects of contemporary politics and were highly regarded by the editor, though Marx considered them merely an unwelcome distraction from his main preoccupation – the drafting of the work on economics for which he had originally signed a contract in Paris in 1845. In spite of repeated assertions that he was on the point of finishing, the work made slow progress in the early 1850s until the prospect of a crisis in 1857 impelled Marx to compose more than eight hundred pages in less than six months. 'I am working madly through the nights,' he wrote to Engels, 'on a synthesis of my economic studies, so that I at least have the main principles clear before the deluge.' This huge manuscript – which became known as the *Grundrisse* (Outlines) – contained notes and excursuses for most of the six parts in which Marx intended to publish the results of his studies. However, Marx was only able to write up the small introductory *Critique of Political Economy* before he was enveloped in a time-consuming polemic with Karl Vogt; and in the early 1860s he could only amass more notes for the historical section of the first part (notes subsequently published under the title *Theories of Surplus Value*). This first part then expanded into the three volumes of *Capital* of which Marx only managed to complete the first, published in 1867 – a work to which Marx declared himself to have 'sacrificed health, happiness and family'. The other two volumes were left in manuscript to be edited by Engels after Marx's death. The other five parts never even got drafted.

The Last Decade

One of the reasons why Marx's work on political economy never got finished was his involvement in the International Workingmen's Association, commonly known as the First International. In 1864 Marx was invited to an international meeting in St Martin's Hall, London; here it was decided to found an International Workingmen's Association whose statutes and *Inaugural Address* were composed by Marx. During the next eight years Marx was the dominant personality on its General Council in London, drafting its various pronouncements on Continental movements, Polish independence as a bulwark against Russian barbarism, support for Irish Home Rule, the shortening of the working day, the transfer of land to common ownership, etc. This work took up the major part of Marx's time. In 1865 he wrote: 'Compared with my work on the book (i.e. *Capital*) the International Association takes up an enormous amount of time, because I am in fact in charge of the whole business.'

The most important political event in the life-time of the International was the Franco-Prussian war and its aftermath. The stability that Europe had enjoyed after the 1848 revolutions was disturbed by the expansionist policy of Prussia under its 'Iron Chancellor' Bismarck. In 1870 Bismarck provoked a war with France in which he very swiftly defeated and captured the Emperor Louis Napoleon. On behalf of the General Council of the International, Marx issued three addresses concerning the war: the first briefly supported the view that the war was one of defence from Germany's point of view and that a French defeat would bring about a revolution in France; the second criticized Prussia for continuing the war after the defeat of Bonaparte, declared that the Prussian annexation of Alsace and Lorraine only sowed the seeds of future war and finally urged the Paris workers to support the provisional government set up on the defeat of Bonaparte. The third address – much the longest, entitled *On the Civil War in France* – was written immediately following the bloody suppression of the rising of the Paris workers against the Provisional government, known as the Paris Commune. Two earlier drafts of this address survive.

The International was seriously weakened by the repression following the Commune and as early as 1870 the split in its ranks caused by the followers of the Russian anarchist Bakunin was already becoming apparent. In as far as they held any coherent doctrine, Bakunin's followers opposed any form of state, even a revolutionary workers' state, called for the equalization of classes, and proposed conspiratorial methods to attain these ends. By 1872 this quarrel had become so serious that Marx was compelled to bring the Association to an end by proposing the transfer of its seat to New York.

In 1869, Engels, who had already been subsidizing Marx to the tune of about £500 a year, decided to sell his partnership in the firm and so could settle an annuity on his friend. While retaining his revolutionary politics, Marx adopted in the 1870s more and more the life-style of a Victorian gentleman to which he had aspired during the two previous decades. Whereas before he had had to pawn 'everything that was not nailed down' in order to keep up appearances in front of the visiting Lassalle, he could now send his daughters to a ladies' seminary, attend continental spas for his health and even boast of gambling on the stock-exchange. The family moved to a large house in Maitland Park Road and Marx was able to play with the children of his two married daughters quite as boisterously as he had played with his own in Dean Street. But in spite of his freedom from financial and domestic worries, the spirit of creative synthesis that had so characterized his work during the two previous decades now deserted him. He had a sort of stroke in 1873 and spent a lot of time travelling in search of health. His work of the 1870s was therefore fragmentary, and he spent most of his working time in taking notes from his still enormous reading and on his wide correspondence. As well as working on the second edition of *Capital* Volume One and its French translation, Marx drew up a detailed criticism of the first common programme of the German socialists who met at Gotha in 1875 at a congress which united the Lassallean wing with the Eisenach party led by Liebknecht and Bebel. These criticisms were published by Engels in 1891 under the title *Critique of the Gotha Programme*. Particularly in his later years Marx began to be very interested in Russia, and among the correspondence of the last years of his life are letters containing a very balanced assessment of the possibilities of Russia's by-passing the capitalist stage of development and basing communism on existing peasant co-operatives.

The end of Marx's life was not a happy one. The death of his wife in 1881 robbed him of all enthusiasm for living and in 1883 his daughter Jenny also died. Two months later, in March 1883, Marx too died, in his armchair.

3 The Thought

The Early Writings

The early writings of Marx are those composed in Germany and Paris up to, and including, 1844. It was not until the composition of *The German Ideology* – in Brussels in 1845/6 – that Marx arrived at the materialistic conception of history that was to be the 'guiding thread' for the rest of his studies. During these early years, Marx's writings show a development through the successive stages of idealism – romantic and then Hegelian – to liberal rationalism and an extended criticism of Hegel's philosophy. Engels said that Marx's ideas were based on a synthesis of German idealist philosophy, French political theory and English classical economics: the early writings show Marx assimilating all three influences – though not, as yet, integrating them.

The intellectual background of Marx's home and school was the rationalism of the Enlightenment, a pale Protestantism incorporating the virtues of reason, moderation and hard work. A radically different perspective was opened up by Baron von Westphalen. Marx's daughter Eleanor wrote that the Baron 'filled Karl Marx with enthusiasm for the romantic school and, whereas his father read Voltaire and Racine with him, the Baron read him Homer and Shakespeare – who remained his favourite authors all his life'. In Bonn, therefore, Marx gave himself up to the current romanticism, though Berlin brought about a decisive change: previously, Hegel's conceptual rationalism had been rejected by Marx, the follower of Kant and Fichte, the romantic subjectivist who considered the highest being to be separate from earthly reality. Now, however, it began to appear to him as though the idea was immanent in the real. Previously Marx had 'read fragments of Hegel's philosophy, but I did not care for its grotesque and rocky melody'. Now he embraced Hegelianism in a conversion that was as profound as it was sudden. It was probably the most important intellectual step of his whole life. For however much he was to criticize Hegel, accuse him of idealism, and try to stand his dialectic 'on its feet', Marx was the first to admit that his method stemmed directly from his master of the 1830s.

Hegel started from the belief that, as he said of the French Revolution, 'man's existence has its centre in his head, i.e. in Reason, under whose inspiration he builds up the world of reality'. In his greatest work, the *Phenomenology*, Hegel traced the development of mind or spirit, reintroducing historical movement into philosophy and asserting that the human mind can attain to absolute knowledge. He analysed the development of human consciousness, from its immediate perception of the here and now, to the stage of self-consciousness, the understanding that allowed man to analyse the world and order his own actions accordingly. Following this was the stage of reason itself, the understanding of the real, after which spirit, by means of religion and art, attained to absolute knowledge, the level at which man recognized in the world the stages of his own reason. These stages Hegel called 'alienations', in so far as they were creations of the human mind yet thought of as independent and superior to the human mind. This absolute knowledge was at the same time a sort of recapitulation of the human spirit, for each successive stage retained elements of the previous ones at the same time as it went beyond them. This movement that suppressed and yet conserved Hegel called *Aufhebung*, a word that has this double sense in German. Hegel also talked of 'the power of the negative', thinking that there was always a tension between any present state of affairs and what it was becoming. For any present state of affairs was in the process of being negated, changed into something else. This process was what Hegel meant by dialectic.

Hegel's philosophy was ambivalent: although he himself preferred to talk of philosophy painting grey with grey and the owl of Minerva only rising at dusk, emphasis on its negative and dialectic side could obviously give it a radical bent – a development associated with a group of intellectuals known as the Young Hegelians. They embarked on a process of secularization, progressing from a critique of religion to one of politics and society. It is important to note that Marx in his early writings is working at his ideas in interaction with the other members of this close-knit movement. His doctoral thesis clearly reflects the Young Hegelian climate: its field – post-Aristotelian Greek philosophy – was one of general interest to the Young Hegelians and Marx's proclamation in the Preface that 'Philosophy makes no secret of it. Prometheus' confession "in a word, I detest all Gods", is its own confession, its own slogan against all Gods in heaven and earth who do not recognize man's self-consciousness as the highest divinity', was typical of the Young Hegelians' anti-religious idealism. The way forward for Marx lay in an application to the 'real' world of the principles that Hegel had discovered.

But Marx did not immediately have the leisure to work on this line of thought: deprived of the possibility of an academic career, his contact with the real world came through his work as a journalist for the *Rheinische Zeitung*. In his seven major articles for the paper, he seldom made his own ideas explicit, since he gave his articles the form of critical exegesis by exposing the absurdities in his opponent's ideas. For this he used any weapon to hand, usually combining a radical Hegelianism with the simple rationalism of the Enlightenment. In October 1842, now as editor, Marx had to reply to the accusation that his paper was flirting with communist ideas. 'The *Rheinische Zeitung*,' he wrote, 'does not even concede theoretical validity to communist ideas in their present form, let alone desires their practical realization'; and he promised a fundamental criticism of such ideas. Soon, however, Marx had to write on such socio-political matters as the law on the thefts of wood and the poverty of the Moselle wine growers – subjects, as he said later, which 'provided the first occasions for occupying myself with economic questions' and impressed on him how closely the laws were formed by the interests of those who were in power.

The eighteen months following the suppression of the *Rheinische Zeitung* were to be decisive for Marx's ideas: in his assault on the metaphysical fog that engulfed not only Hegel but also much Young Hegelian writing, Marx was helped by two things. Firstly, he was reading a lot of politics and history: he read French Socialism even before he went to Paris and his reading in the French Revolution was extensive. Indeed, his writing of this period can be viewed as an extended meditation on the question of why the French Revolution, which started out with such excellent principles, had yet failed to solve the fundamental problem of the redistribution of social wealth. Secondly, there was the influence of Ludwig Feuerbach. Although Engels exaggerated when he said later that 'we all became Feuerbachians', this influence was profound. Feuerbach was fundamentally interested in religion and his main thesis was that God was merely a projection of human attributes, desires and potentialities. If men once realized this, they would be in a position to appropriate these attributes for themselves by realizing that they had created God, not God them, and thus be in a position to restore to themselves their alienated 'species-being' or communal essence. What interested Marx was the application of this approach to Hegel's philosophy, which Feuerbach regarded as the last bulwark of theology in that Hegel

27

still started from the ideal instead of the real. Feuerbach wrote: 'The true relationship of thought to being is this: being is the subject, thought the predicate. Thought arises from being – being does not arise from thought.'

This view of Feuerbach was incorporated into a long manuscript that Marx composed in the summer of 1843. Here, by means of a critique of Hegel, Marx's views on democracy and the abolition of the state began to take shape. According to Hegel's political philosophy, human consciousness manifested itself objectively in man's juridical, social and political institutions which alone permitted man to attain to full liberty. Only the highest level of social organization – the State – was capable of uniting particular rights and universal reason. Hegel thus rejected the view that man was free by nature: on the contrary, for him the state was the only means of making man's freedom real. In other words, Hegel was aware of the social problems created by a competitive society in which there was an economic war of all against all – a state of affairs which he summed up under the term 'Civil Society'; but he considered that these conflicts could be harmonized by the organs of the state into some 'higher' unity. Following Feuerbach, Marx's fundamental criticism of Hegel was that, as in religion men had imagined God to be the creator and man to be dependent on Him, so Hegel mistakenly started from the Idea of the State and made everything else – the family and various social groups – dependent on this Idea. Applying this general approach to particular issues, Marx declared himself in favour of democracy: 'Just as religion does not create man, but man creates religion, so the constitution does not create the people but the people the constitution.' Marx was especially concerned, in a few pages of brilliant analysis, to reject Hegel's view that the bureaucracy performed a mediating function between different social groups and thus acted as a 'universal class' in the interests of all. Marx considered that bureaucracy encouraged the political divisions that were essential to its own existence and thus pursued its own ends to the detriment of the community at large. Towards the end of his manuscript, Marx described how he expected universal suffrage to inaugurate the reform of civil society by bringing back to it the social essence of man as a communal being that had been stolen from him and transferred to the sphere of constitutions that had no effect on his real life.

The manuscript on Hegel was never published, but the embryonic ideas it contained received a clearer formulation when Marx got to Paris. During the winter of 1843/4 Marx wrote two essays for the *Deutsch-französische Jahrbücher* – both as clear and sparkling as the Hegel manuscript had been involved and obscure. In the first, entitled *On the Jewish Question*, Marx reviewed the opinions of his old mentor Bruno Bauer on Jewish emancipation. According to Bauer, for Jewish emancipation to be effective, the state had to cease to be Christian – otherwise discrimination against the Jews was inevitable. But for Marx, Bauer had not gone far enough: for the mere secularization of politics did not entail the emancipation of men as human beings. The United States had no established religion, yet was notorious for the religiosity of its inhabitants. Marx continued:

> But since the existence of religion is the existence of a defect, the source of this defect can only be sought in the nature of the state itself. Religion for us no longer has the force of a basis for secular deficiencies but only that of a phenomenon. We do not change secular questions into theological ones. We change theological questions into secular ones. History has for long enough been resolved into superstition: we now resolve superstition into history. The question of the relationship of political emancipation to religion becomes for us a question of the relationship of political emancipation to human emancipation.

In Marx's view this problem arose because 'man has a life both in the political community, where he is valued as a communal being, and in civil society where he is active as a private individual, treats other men as means, degrades himself to a means and becomes the plaything of alien powers'.

Bauer had argued for a state based exclusively on the universal rights of man as proclaimed by the French Revolution and the American Declaration of Independence. For Marx, however, the rights of man were only the rights of the atomized, mutually hostile individuals of civil society. Thus

> the right of man to freedom is not based on the union of man with man, but on the separation of man from man . . . The right of man to property is the right to enjoy his possessions and dispose of the same arbitrarily, without regard for other men, independently of society, the right of selfishness. It is the former individual freedom together with its latter application that forms the basis of civil society. It leads man to see in other men not the realization but the limitation of his own freedom.

After pointing out that the society inaugurated by the French Revolution had forfeited many of the social and communal dimensions present in feudal society, Marx sketched his goal of bridging the gap between the individual viewed as a citizen member of a community and as an isolated egoistic member of civil society:

> The actual individual man must take the abstract citizen back into himself and, as an individual man in his empirical life, in his individual work and individual relationships, become a species-being; man must recognize his own forces as social forces, organize them and thus no longer separate social forces from himself in the form of political forces. Only when this has been achieved will human emancipation be completed.

The article *On the Jewish Question* had set the goal of full human emancipation; in his second article for the *Jahrbücher* Marx identified the means to achieve it. This article was intended as an introduction to his critique of Hegel which was to be written up for publication. The article began with Marx's famous epigrams on religion:

> The foundation of irreligious criticism is this: man makes religion, religion does not make man. But man is no abstract being squatting outside the world. Man is the world of man, the state, society. This state, this society, produces religion's inverted attitude to the world, because they are an inverted world themselves. Thus the struggle against religion is indirectly the struggle against that world whose spiritual aroma is religion ... Religion is the sigh of the oppressed creature, the feeling of a heartless world, and the soul of soulless circumstances. It is the opium of the people ...

But the role of religion having been exposed, the duty of philosophers was now to direct their attention to politics, a particularly appropriate activity in a Germany which was, according to Marx, still pre-1789. The one hope for Germany lay in her political philosophy, which was very progressive: the Germans had *thought* what other nations had *done*. So to criticize this philosophy and progress beyond it would show, at least theoretically, what the future of society was to be. And although Marx was clear that 'the criticism of religion ends with the doctrine that man is the highest being for man, that is, with the categorical imperative to overthrow all circumstances in which man is humiliated, enslaved, abandoned and despised', the difficulty obviously lay in finding 'a passive element, a material basis' necessary to revolution. He proclaimed the solution in a passage that has given much support to the view of Marx as a messianic, prophetic figure. The solution lay

> ... in the formation of a class with radical chains, a

class in civil society that is not a class of civil society, of a social group that is the dissolution of all social groups, of a sphere that has a universal character because of its universal sufferings and lays claim to no particular right, because it is the object of no particular injustice but of injustice in general. This class can no longer lay claim to a historical status, but only to a human one. It is, finally, a sphere that cannot emancipate itself without emancipating these other spheres themselves. In a word, it is the complete loss of humanity and thus can only recover itself by a complete redemption of humanity. This dissolution of society, as a particular class, is the proletariat . . .

Thus the vehicle of revolution was clear to Marx: the proletariat was destined to assume the universal role that Hegel had misleadingly assigned to the bureaucracy. But hitherto Marx's writings had been almost exclusively political, although he had come to realize that politics was not enough: his interest in the essential economic dimension was sparked off by an essay published in the *Deutsch-französische Jahrbücher* alongside his own two. It was by Friedrich Engels and entitled *Outlines of a Critique of Political Economy*. In it, Engels indicted private property and its concomitant spirit of competition. Growing capitalist accumulation necessarily entailed a lowering of salaries and accentuated the class struggle. Uncurtailed growth of the economy meant recurrent crises and the progress of science only served to increase the misery of the workers. This 'sketch of genius' (as he later called it) made a great impression on Marx and his notebooks during the summer of 1844 begin with extracts from it. These notes (unpublished by Marx) were entitled by their first editors 'Economic and Philosophical Manuscripts' (EPM) and represent a radical critique of capitalism based partly on Engels, partly on the anti-industrial ideas of such German romantics as Schiller and partly on Feuerbach's humanism. On their first full publication in 1932 they were hailed by some as Marx's most important single piece of work (see below, Chapter 4).

The EPM consist of three main sections: a critique of the classical economists culminating with a section on alienated labour; a description of communism; and a critique of Hegel's dialectic.

The first of these sections contains lengthy quotations from the classical economists – in particular Smith and Ricardo – to demonstrate the increasing polarization of classes and the deleterious effects of private property. Although he considered that the economists faithfully reported the workings of capitalist society, Marx criticized their approach on three main grounds: firstly, while admitting that labour was fundamental to the working of the economy, they acquiesced in assigning to it an increasingly poverty-stricken role; secondly, they did not view the economic system as one of interacting forces, that is, they took the laws of capitalism to be immutable and could not explain the origins of the system they were describing; thirdly, they took a one-sided view of man simply as a cog in the economic wheel and did not consider him 'in his free time, as a human being'.

At this point Marx began a new section headed 'alienated labour' and containing a description of the general impoverishment and dehumanization of the worker in capitalist society. Alienated labour had four aspects to it. Firstly, the worker was related to the product of his labour as to an alien object; it stood over and above him, opposed to him as an independent power. Secondly, the worker became alienated from himself in the very act of production; for the worker did not view his work as part of his real life and did not feel at home in it. Thirdly, man's 'species-life', his social essence, was taken away from him in his work which did not represent the harmonious efforts of man as a 'species-being'. Fourthly, man found himself alienated from other men.

In an extended note on James Mill written about this time (unfortunately not included in most editions of the EPM), Marx attacked the notion of credit which he called 'the economic judgement on the morality of a man. In credit, man himself, instead of metal or paper, has become the mediator of exchange but not as man, but as the existence of capital and interest'. In contemporary society, according to Marx, men were increasingly producing with the sole object of exchanging and thus 'you have no relation to my object as a human being because I myself have no human relation to it . . . our mutual value is the value of our objects for us'. The passage towards the end of the note constitutes a sort of positive counterpart to the description of alienated labour and deserves quoting in full:

> Supposing that we had produced in a human manner; each of us would in his production have doubly affirmed himself and his fellow men. I would have: (1) objectified in my production my individuality and its peculiarity and thus both in my activity enjoyed an individual expression of my life and also in looking at the object have had the individual pleasure of realizing that my personality was objective, visible to the senses and thus a power raised beyond all doubt. (2) In your enjoyment or use of my product I would have had the direct enjoyment of realizing that I had both satisfied a human need by my work and also objectified the human essence and therefore fashioned for another human being the object that met his need. (3) I would have been for you the mediator between you and the species and thus been acknowledged and felt by you as a completion of your own essence and a necessary part of yourself and have thus realized that I am confirmed both in your thought and in your love. (4) In my expression of my life I would have fashioned your expression of your life, and thus

in my own activity have realized my own essence, my human, my communal essence.

The second main section of the EPM contained Marx's solution to the problem of alienation in communism. Although while still in Germany he had rejected communism as a 'dogmatic and one-sided abstraction', the impact of Paris had made him a swift convert. But Marx's communism was not the 'crude' kind, inspired by 'universal envy', that aimed to negate all culture in a levelling-down process. He summarized his ideas in an almost mystical passage:

> . . . communism as the positive abolition of private property and thus of human self-alienation and therefore the real reappropriation of the human essence by and for man. This is communism as the complete and conscious return of man himself as a social, i.e. human being. Communism as completed naturalism is humanism and as completed humanism is naturalism. It is the genuine solution of the antagonism between man and nature and between man and man. It is the true solution of the struggle between existence and essence, between objectification and self-affirmation, between freedom and necessity, between individual and species. It is the solution to the riddle of history and knows itself to be this solution.

In the following sections (in many ways the key passage of the EPM), Marx expanded on three particular aspects of his conception of communism. Firstly, he stressed that communism was a *historical* phenomenon whose genesis was 'the entire movement of history'. At the present stage, the essential problem was an economic one – in particular the abolition of private property: 'the positive abolition of private property and the appropriation of human life is the positive abolition of all alienation, thus the return of man from religion, family, state, etc., to his human, that is, social being.' Secondly, Marx stressed that everything about man – starting with his language – was *social*. Even man's relationship to nature was included in this social dimension:

> thus society completes the essential unity of man with nature, it is the genuine resurrection of nature, the fulfilled naturalism of man and humanism of nature . . . For not only the five senses but also the so-called spiritual and moral senses (will, love, etc.), in a word, human love and the humanity of the senses come into being only through the existence of their object, through nature humanized. The development of the five senses is a labour of the whole previous history of the world.

Nevertheless Marx was to emphasize, thirdly, that the stress on man's social aspects only served to enhance the *individuality* of communist, unalienated man whom he described as 'total' or 'all-sided'. For just as the state of alienation vitiated all human faculties, so the supersession of this alienation would be a total liberation. It would not just be limited to the possession and enjoyment of material objects: all human faculties would, in their different ways, become means of appropriating reality. This was difficult to imagine for alienated man, since private property had so blunted men's sensibility that they could only imagine an object to be theirs when they actually possessed it: all physical and intellectual senses had been replaced by the single alienation of *having*. And, finally, the reciprocal relationship between man and nature would be reflected in a single all-embracing science; 'natural science will in time comprise the science of man, as the science of man will embrace natural science: there will be one single science'.

The third and final section of the EPM was devoted to a critique of Hegel's dialectic as found in his most famous work, the *Phenomenology of Spirit*. Marx began by praising Feuerbach for having shown that Hegel's philosophy was no more than a rationalized theology and discovering the true materialist approach by starting from the social relationship of man to man. But Marx's attitude to Hegel was far from being wholly negative:

> The greatness of Hegel's *Phenomenology* and its final product, the dialectic of negativity as the moving and creating principle, is on the one hand that Hegel conceives of the self-creation of man as a process, objectification as loss of the object, as externalisation and the transcendence of this externalisation. This means, therefore, that he grasps the nature of labour and understands objective man, true because real, man as the result of his own labour.

But on the other hand this whole dialectic was viewed from an idealist standpoint: 'The appropriation of man's objectified and alienated faculties, is thus first only an appropriation that occurs in the mind, in pure thought, i.e. in abstraction.' Marx, however, started from the 'real man of flesh and blood, standing on the solid round earth and breathing in and out all the powers of nature' and defined his position as a consistent naturalism or humanism that avoided both idealism and materialism. Hegel saw man as a disembodied consciousness and the world as necessarily inimical to man's fulfilment. Marx, on the other hand, considered that it was only man's present relationship to the world that was askew: man needed to interact with external objects in order to develop or 'objectify' himself. For Hegel, all objectification was alienation; for Marx, man could only overcome alienation if he objectified himself by using nature in co-operation with his fellow men.

With his move to Brussels in 1845 Marx's writings take on a systematic form – albeit as an open-ended system – that is not present in his early writings. These early writings document Marx's struggle to conclude, from very idealistic beginnings, that the fundamental activity of man was one of productive interchange with nature; that this activity was vitiated by the class divisions of capitalist society with its institutions of private property and the division of labour; and that this present alienation could be overcome by a proletarian revolution inaugurating communism.

History

The fact that Marx never used the expression 'historical materialism' (still less 'dialectical materialism') is not merely a linguistic point: it indicates the open-ended nature of his approach to history which he preferred to call 'the materialist conception of history'. The key to this approach was the idea (central to the EPM) that the essential element in an understanding of man and his history was a comprehension of man's productive activity. The fundamental activity of man was the way he obtained his means of subsistence by interaction with nature – in short, his labour. Marx summed up in *Capital* his view of labour as the instrument of man's self-creation:

> Labour is a process in which both man and nature participate, and in which man of his own accord starts, regulates and controls the material reactions between himself and nature . . . By thus acting on the external world and changing it, he at the same time changes his own nature. He develops his slumbering powers and compels them to act in obedience to his sway.

This self-creation through labour was the primary factor in history and the ideas and concepts – political, philosophical or religious – through which men interpreted this activity were secondary. For history was not the result of accident, nor was it shaped by the acts of great men (and still less supernatural powers): history was the – mostly unconscious – creation of labouring men and subject to observable laws.

Perhaps the most vital point in any understanding of Marx is that when he called himself a materialist what he meant was quite simply that in order to understand man it was essential to begin with the material conditions of his production. Thus Marx was not an empiricist: he did not believe that insight could be got from a collection of dead facts; he drew a distinction between essence and appearance; and he poured considerable scorn on 'common sense' which he considered as poor a guide in history and economics as it would be to the question of whether the earth moved round the sun. Nor was Marx a materialist in the rather metaphysical sense of someone who believes that the world consists only of matter. Indeed, Marx's most detailed account of his materialist conception of history was contained in *The German Ideology*, which was intended to distinguish his views from those of Feuerbach on precisely this question. His main point – summarized trenchantly in the accompanying *Theses on Feuerbach* – was that man was *not* simply a product of material conditions: such a view left out the subjective, creative side of man's interaction with nature. Taking to task the French materialists of the eighteenth century, Marx wrote that 'the materialist doctrine concerning the changing of circumstances and upbringing forgets that circumstances are made by men and the educator must himself be educated'. What Marx was concerned centrally to deny was the validity of any doctrine that claimed to be able to give an 'objective', neutral or static account of the world from an uninvolved position. Thus 'the question whether objective truth can be attributed to human thinking is not a question of theory but a *practical* question'. In order to attain to this 'neutral' view a man would have to be outside society – just as Archimedes's firm point from which to start his system of levers would have had to be outside the world. But no one could get outside society, no more than Archimedes could get outside the world. Since, therefore, everyone spoke from a point of view, the eleventh, and best known, thesis was mandatory on all: 'Philosophers have only *interpreted* the world, in various ways; the point is to *change* it.'

There are in the later Marx certain traces of positivism and he was certainly not immune to the general enthusiasm for a supposedly value-free natural science that reached its high point in late Victorian society. But the general view (obviously derived from Hegel) that no element in the total process of history could be isolated and given a significance unaffected by the other elements – this view stayed with Marx throughout his life.

Marx's ideas are often referred to as 'the economic interpretation of history'. The clearest statement of the importance Marx attached to economics is contained in the *Preface* to the *Critique of Political Economy*. Here Marx stated that:

> In the social production of their life, men enter into definite relations that are indispensable and independent of their will, relations of production which correspond to a definite state of development of their material productive forces. The sum total of these relations of production constitutes the economic structure of society, the real foundation, on which rises a legal and political superstructure and to which correspond definite forms of social consciousness. The mode of production of material life conditions the social, political and intellectual life process in general. It is not the consciousness of men that determines their being, but, on the contrary, their social being that determines their consciousness. At a certain stage of their development, the material productive forces of society come in conflict with the existing relations of production, or – what is but a legal expression for the same thing – with the property relations within which they have been at work hitherto. From forms of development of the productive forces these relations turn into their fetters. Then begins an epoch of social revolution.

There were, of course, elements in Marx's thought that tended to overemphasize aspects of necessity and predetermination in his view of society. Engels wrote later:

> Marx and I are ourselves partly to blame for the fact that the younger people sometimes lay more stress on the economic side than is due to it. We had to emphasize the main principle vis-à-vis our adversaries, who denied it, and we had not always the time, the place or the opportunity to give their due to the other elements involved in the interaction.

In consequence, some interpreters have read into the above quotation a kind of economic determinism, supposing Marx to have said that other elements in the historical process were uniquely determined by the economic one; or even that the only important economic factor was the actual instruments of production. It is true that Marx sometimes narrowed down the determining factor in such statements as 'the hand mill will give you a society with the feudal lord, the steam engine a society with the industrial capitalist'. It has been strongly argued in criticism of Marx that any theory of historical materialism which separates the base from the superstructure was invalid, since the base necessarily involved elements from the superstructure – for example, it is impossible to conceive of any economic organization of society without some concept of rules and obligations. But it is doubtful whether Marx ever formulated his theory as the strict causal one implied by this criticism. The most that could be said is that for Marx technological change was a necessary, though not a sufficient, condition of social change. Nor is the language used to describe the relationship of the base to the superstructure always precise: sometimes Marx uses the term 'determine', sometimes the milder 'condition', sometimes again the phrase 'correspond to' – which conveys a rather different idea. Thus Marx's theory is best regarded as intended to supply a series of flexible structural concepts through which to interpret the development of past and present societies.

It is also clear that Marx assigned a positive role to non-economic factors in society. Indeed, he sometimes included the workers themselves among the instruments of production and even called the revolutionary class 'the greatest productive power of all the instruments of production'. It is significant that in the above quotation from the *Preface* what is said to determine consciousness is not simply 'being' but *'social* being'. Yet ideas, for Marx, were definitely of secondary importance in the understanding of society. He warned that, just as we would be chary of judging an individual by what he thought of himself, so we should not rely on the self-interpretation of a particular epoch. To take a particular example, the rights of man as proclaimed in the French Revolution and the constitution of the United States were not eternal truths about the nature of man which happened to be discovered at that particular time – as those who proclaimed them imagined; they could only be fully understood if viewed in the context of demands by new commercial groups for the end of feudal restrictions and for free competition in economic affairs. It was in this sense of ideas propagated to serve a particular class interest that Marx usually used the term 'ideology'.

Marx would have been the first to agree that his own ideas were in some sense ideological in that they, too, were destined to serve a class interest. But he would have equally insisted that although his ideas could not claim objective and static truth, they were nevertheless valid in terms of the point of view from which they stemmed and which they articulated – that of the proletariat. This position throws some light on the difficult question of whether Marx's views imply an ethical standpoint. The answer (though not a very satisfactory one for those who believe in a sharp distinction between fact and value) is that Marx does have an ethical standpoint, but not one that is describable in isolation from his statements on society and history. For example, Marx *does* have a concept of human nature – but not a static one which, as in many previous political philosophers, would act as an easy yardstick from which to read off recommendations about society. Marx's labouring, productive man is constantly developing and changing his relationship to the world and thereby changing – creating – his own nature.

This self-creation of man (albeit under determined circumstances) is central for Marx. Thus the instruments of production can never be isolated from their social context. The core of the Marxian dialectic is the unity of subjective and objective factors that is present, to some extent, throughout history and increasingly so as the revolution approaches.

History does nothing; it does not possess immense riches, it does not fight battles. It is men, real, living men, who do all this, who possess things and fight battles. It is not 'history' which uses men as a means of achieving – as if it were an individual person – its own ends. History is nothing but the activity of men in pursuit of their ends.

Or again:

Men make their own history, but they do not make it just as they please; they do not make it under circumstances chosen by themselves, but under circumstances directly encountered, given and transmitted from the past.

The most important concept in Marx that mediated the subjective and objective sides of the dialectic was that of class. Classes were the basic social groups by means of whose conflict society developed in accordance with changes in its economic substructure. The opening words of *The Communist Manifesto* were: 'The history of all hitherto existing societies is the history of class struggles.' Unfortunately, Marx nowhere offers a systematic analysis of the concept of class. But it is clear that the role played by classes is a compound of subjective and objective factors.

On the objective side, an obvious question is: how many classes are there? There is the beginning of an answer at the end of *Capital*, Volume III, where Marx stated that, in terms of identity of revenues and sources of revenue, there were three great social classes – wage-labourers, capitalists and landowners; but the manuscript broke off just as Marx was putting the crucial question as to why doctors, lawyers, etc., were not therefore separate classes. Marx often used a model consisting of only two classes: this model is present in the *Communist Manifesto* where Marx wrote that 'society as a whole is more and more splitting up into two great classes directly facing each other: bourgeoisie and proletariat': and the same view reappears in *Capital*. Here the criterion for belonging to a class is ownership or non-ownership of the means of production. It should be emphasized (particularly when discussing the two class models) that Marx was thinking in terms of trends and projected into the future tendencies that he saw in contemporary society. One of the most important of these trends was the immiserization of the proletariat. Marx was usually chary of claiming that the proletariat would become immiserized in any absolute sense. Such an idea would not have harmonized well with his view of all human needs as mediated through society. What he did claim was that the gap in resources between those who owned the means of production and those who did not would widen.

In contemporary comment Marx used the term 'class' of several social groups. In Britain, Marx talked of 'the ruling classes', and he even went so far as to say that finance capitalists and industrial capitalists 'form two distinct classes'. At the other end of the social scale was what Marx called the *Lumpen-proletariat*, whom Marx described as 'a recruiting ground for thieves and criminals of all kinds, living on the crumbs of society, people without a definite trade, vagabonds, people without a hearth or a home'. In other words the *Lumpen-proletariat* were the drop-outs of society who had no stake in the development of society and so no historical role to play – except occasionally to sell their services to the bourgeoisie. A particular problem for the two-class model was the peasantry. Although Marx's normal characterization of the proletariat only applied to industrial workers, yet sometimes he spoke of the proletariat as comprising the vast majority of the people in capitalist society and so, presumably, as including farm labourers; and in a comment on Bakunin in 1875 he spoke of the possibility of a situation in which 'the capitalist tenant has ousted the peasants, and the real tiller of the soil is just as much a proletarian, a wage worker, as is the urban worker and thus shares with him interests that are directly the same'. He also, in the same comment, says that sometimes even the land-owning peasant belongs to the proletariat, though he is not conscious of it: the burden of mortgage on his land means that he does not really own it and is, in effect, working for someone else. Thus if the peasants are held to be proletarians and the landowners to be capitalists, the two class model is again in force. There are also indications in some of Marx's later unpublished writings that he took into account the growth of the middle classes and the increasing importance in society of the service industries – but these factors were not given any systematic treatment.

Equally important in Marx's view of class was the subjective or dynamic element: a class only existed when it was conscious of itself as such, and this always implied common hostility to another social group. Thus Marx was sometimes hesitant as to whether even the capitalists formed a class in the full sense of the word. He wrote of them: 'the separate individuals form a class in so far as they have to carry on a common battle against another class; otherwise they are on hostile terms with each other as competitors.' The same applied to the proletariat: Marx spoke of times when 'the proletariat is not yet sufficiently developed to constitute itself into a class', and said of the proletariat that 'this mass is already a class in opposition to capital, but not yet a class for itself'. And in the *Communist Manifesto* he declared that 'this organization of the proletarians into a class, and consequently into a political party, is continually being upset again by the competition between the workers themselves': and as late as 1866 Marx talked of the International as an instrument for 'the organization of the workers into a class'. The clearest account of the subjective element in class is Marx's description of the French peasantry:

> In so far as millions of families live under economic conditions of existence that separate their mode of life, their interests and their culture from those of the other classes and put them in hostile opposition to the latter, they form a class. In so far as there is merely a local interconnection among those small-holding peasants and the identity of their interests begets no community, no national bond, and no political organization among them, they do not form a class. They are consequently incapable of enforcing their class interest in their own name . . .

Engels once advised a correspondent who had enquired about historical materialism to read Marx's comments on contemporary history such as *The Eighteenth Brumaire*. In order to emphasize the flexibility of Marx's approach to history it is worth considering in rather more detail two 'case studies': his comments on the relation of art to socio-economic factors and the possible future development of Russian society.

At the end of the General Introduction to the *Grundrisse*, Marx noted a number of points that he intended to deal with later; one of these was 'the unequal relation between the development of material production and art, for instance'. In other words, 'certain periods of the highest development of art stand in no direct connection to the general development of society, or to the material basis and skeleton structure of its organization'. For example, Greek mythology was the basis of Greek art; but the view of nature and social relations which had shaped Greek imagination and art was not possible in an age of automatic machinery, locomotives and electricity. What, asked Marx, became of the Goddess Fama when faced with Printing House Square? Or how was Achilles possible side by side with powder and lead? Thus the problem was in understanding why Greek art 'still constitutes for us a source of aesthetic enjoyment and in certain respects prevails as the standard and model beyond attainment'. Marx's answer to this question was: 'Why should the childhood of human society, where it has attained its most beautiful development, not exert an eternal charm as an age that will never return?' This answer is certainly an unsatisfactory one; but the discussion shows that Marx was well aware that his theory could not necessarily yield any ready-made answers to historical problems.

The second example is Marx's view of Russian development. In 1877 Mikhailovsky, one of the leading Russian Populist theoreticians, attacked Marx's ideas by claiming that *Capital* involved a condemnation of the efforts of Russians who worked for a development in their country which would by-pass the capitalist stage. In reply Marx insisted on the possibility of Russia's avoiding the capitalist stage and attacked Mikhailovsky who 'absolutely must metamorphose my historical sketch of the genesis of capitalism in Western Europe into a historico-philosophical theory of the general path every people is fated to tread, whatever the historical circumstances in which it finds itself . . .', and criticized any approach which tried to understand history 'by using as one's master key a general historico-philosophical theory, the supreme virtue of which consists in being supra-historical'.

Marx returned again to this question in 1881 when the Russian Marxist Vera Sassoulitch asked him to clarify his views.

> Lately [she wrote] we often hear it said that the rural commune is an archaic form condemned to perish by history, scientific socialism and all that is least subject to debate. The people who preach this call themselves your disciples *par excellence*: 'Marxists'. The strongest of their arguments is often: 'Marx has said it.' 'But how do you deduce it from his *Capital*? He does not discuss the agrarian problem nor Russia,' was the objection. Your disciples reply: 'he would have said it had he talked of our country.'

Marx's short reply was enigmatic:

> The analysis given in *Capital* does not offer any reasons either for or against the vitality of the rural commune, but the special study that I have made of it, for which I have researched the material in its original sources, has convinced me that this commune is the starting point for the social regeneration of Russia, but that, in order for it to function as such, it would be necessary first of all to eliminate the deleterious influences that assail it on all sides and then to assure it the normal conditions for a spontaneous development.

Brief though Marx's reply was, it was based on three very lengthy drafts which thoroughly analysed the development of the peasant commune and contained the more optimistic conclusion that:

> To save the Russian commune, a Russian revolution is necessary. Moreover, the Russian Government and the

'new pillars of society' are doing their best to prepare the masses for such a catastrophe. If the revolution comes at an opportune moment, if it concentrates all its forces to ensure the free development of the rural commune, this commune will soon develop into an element that regenerates Russian society and guarantees superiority over countries enslaved by the capitalist regime.

Thus Marx's view on this question so crucial to the development of Marxism was fatefully ambivalent.

These two case studies illustrate the flexibility of Marx's approach to history – an approach that was always informed by the dialectical unity of subjective and objective factors that lay at the centre of his views.

Economics

In his best-known formulation of the materialist conception of history, Marx wrote that

in the social production of their life, men enter into definite relations that are indispensable and independent of their will, relations of production which correspond to a definite stage of development of their material productive forces.

Marx's economic doctrines are embedded in this conception of history in that they aim to analyse the relations of production and corresponding material productive forces in bourgeois society – 'to lay bare the economic law of modern society', as he wrote in the 'Preface' to *Capital*. That Marx's economics cannot be separated from his sociology, his politics or his history can be seen from *Capital* itself whose first volume is by no means as drily economic as is sometimes thought: more than half the book is an extremely readable application of the materialist conception of history to contemporary British capitalism. The wealth of detail and vividness of style demonstrate both the meticulousness of his research and his great literary talent. Nevertheless, as Marx himself said, every beginning is difficult and *Capital* is no exception. Before offering a brief description of Marx's main economic doctrines a few remarks on the nature of Marx's approach are necessary – all the more so as much interest has focused recently on Marx's methodology.

The two main places where Marx describes his method are the 'General Introduction' to the *Grundrisse* and the 'Preface' to the Second Edition of *Capital*. These passages are also crucial for an understanding of what Marx owed to Hegel. Marx says here that the researcher begins by having before him the chaotic mass of his subject-matter – in this case modern bourgeois society. He then breaks it down into its constituent elements and arrives at ever more simple and abstract concepts, each of which, however, only has full meaning by reference to all the others. Only after this analysis can the process of conceptual synthesis begin, a process in which the whole is built up again, starting from the most abstract and simple concepts – in this case, value, labour, and so on. Thus the scientific researcher into economics starts with the chaotic apprehension of bourgeois society, analyses it conceptually by empirical study into its most abstract constituent elements, and then proceeds to synthesize these elements through a dialectical exposition to yield a total conceptual comprehension of the object under study. In essence, this is Hegel's method with the proviso that in Hegel the place of the correct method of analysis and synthesis is taken by the Idea conceived of as an autonomous subject. Hegel had grasped the necessity of moving from the abstract to the concrete but had at the same time mystified his approach by starting with the Idea instead of the empirical content. This is what Marx meant by the famous phrase about having found Hegel standing on his head and put him back on his feet. 'My relationship to Hegel is very simple,' Marx wrote,

> I am a disciple of Hegel and the presumptuous chattering of the *epigoni* who believe they have buried this eminent thinker seems to me frankly to be ridiculous. However that may be, I have taken the liberty of adopting a critical attitude towards my master, to rid his dialectic of its mysticism and thus to subject it to a profound change.

But though Marx's methodology may have been Hegelian, the concepts with which he was operating were part of a longer tradition – that of the classical economists, and in particular Adam Smith and David Ricardo. It was this combination that led Lassalle to describe Marx as a 'Hegel turned economist and a Ricardo turned socialist'. In a sense, Marx was the last and the greatest of the classical economists. For the concepts that he used were part of the language common to all economists in the mid-nineteenth century but thereafter abandoned by the orthodox schools of economics. Since the third quarter of the nineteenth century, economists in Western Europe and America have tended to look at the capitalist system as given, construct models of it, assuming private property, profit and a more or less free market, and to discuss the functionings of this model, concentrating particularly on prices. This 'marginalist' school of economics has no concept of value apart from price. To Marx, this procedure seemed superficial for two reasons: firstly, he considered it superficial in a literal sense, in that it was only a description of phenomena lying on the surface of capitalist society without an analysis of the mode of production that gave rise to these phenomena. Secondly, this approach took the capitalist system for granted whereas Marx wished to analyse 'the birth, life and death of a given social organism and its replacement by another, superior order'.

Central to the classical theory had been the labour theory of value according to which the value of objects was measured by the amount of labour embodied in them. This fitted in well with the general view of Marx that socially productive labour was the basic factor in economic life. Marx distinguished between use-value and exchange-value. In former times use-value had been important and objects were exchanged for each other either directly or through the intermediary of money. But under capitalism the ultimate aim was to turn commodities into money. And the commodity 'whose use-value possesses the peculiar property of being a source of value, whose actual consumption, therefore, is itself an embodiment of labour and, consequently, a creation of value' was 'the capacity for labour or labour power'.

But this labour theory of value seemed to involve the puzzle that in the exchange of capital and labour the wages of the labourer had a smaller exchange-value than the exchange value of the object he produced. Marx accounted for this phenomenon of profit by means of his theory of surplus-value which was characterized by Engels as Marx's most important 'discovery' in economics. Marx made a distinction between *constant* capital which was 'that part of capital which is represented by the means of production, by the raw material, auxiliary material and instruments of labour, and does not, in the process of production, undergo any quantitative alteration of value' and *variable* capital. Of this Marx said:

> That part of capital, represented by labour power, does, in the process of production, undergo an alteration of value. It both reproduces the equivalent of its own value, and also produces an excess, a surplus value, which may itself vary, may be more or less according to the circumstances.

(It is important to note that Marx talked here of labour *power* – a refinement he introduced into his theory during the 1850s. For plainly, if the exchange value of a commodity equalled the amount of labour incorporated in it, the exchange-value of a day's labour must be equal to its product, i.e., the wages of the labourer will be the same as his product.) The essential point was that the capitalist got the worker to work longer than was merely sufficient to embody in his product the value of his labour power. For example, if the value of the labour power of the worker (roughly what it cost to keep him and his family alive and capable of working) was £4 a day and if he could embody £4 of value in the product of his work during four hours: then, if he worked eight hours, the second half of his day would yield surplus-value – in this case £4. The variation in surplus-value mentioned above was called the rate of surplus-value (or rate of exploitation) around which the struggle between capitalists and workers centred. The capitalists were constantly trying to increase the rate of surplus-value by either extending the hours of labour, or making the labour more intensive or more productive. This production of a surplus was not confined to capitalism, but previously the surplus had simply been appropriated by the possessing class. In capitalism, this appropriation was concealed by the apparently free market bargain by the capitalists and workers who seemed to be merely exchanging equivalents.

The theory of surplus value also had implications for the long-term future of capitalism. These were: for the capitalists, that their rate of profit would decrease; for the workers, that their relative standard of living would decline; and for the capitalist system as a whole, that it would be shaken by a series of crises that would culminate in a transition to communism.

The tendency for the rate of profit to decline was due, according to Marx, to changes in what he called the organic composition of capital – the ratio of constant to variable capital. Competition among capitalists and technological progress would increase the amount of capital invested in machines as opposed to that paid out in wages. And since it was only labour that produced a surplus, this meant that profits would fall – always supposing that the rate of surplus-value remained unchanged. Marx realized that the tendency for profits to decline could be offset by raising the rate of surplus value either by increasing labour's productivity or intensity, or by cheapening the cost of raw materials through colonial expansion. But he considered that these were only short-term palliatives which could not prevent the eventual destruction of the system.

For the workers, Marx foresaw a relative decline in their standard of living in that the proportion of the gross national product accruing to the working class would get less – although, of course, wages might well rise in real terms. For the competition among capitalists was paralleled by competition among workers who were constantly threatened with replacement from the 'industrial reserve army' or mass of unemployed. This tended to prevent real wages from rising very much above subsistence level for any considerable length of time. In *Capital* Marx paints a grim picture of the fate of the working class:

Within the capitalist system all methods for raising the social productiveness of labour are brought about at the cost of the individual labourer; all means for the development of production transform themselves into means of domination over, and exploitation of, the producers; they mutilate the labourer into a fragment of a man, degrade him to the level of an appendage of a machine, destroy every remnant of charm in his work and turn it into a hated toil; they estrange from him the intellectual potentialities of the labour-process in the same proportion as science is incorporated in it as an independent power; they distort the conditions under which he works, subject him during the labour-process to a despotism the more hateful for its meanness; they transform his lifetime into working-time, and drag his wife and child beneath the wheels of the Juggernaut of capital.

In other of his writings, however, Marx is less pessimistic about the effects of capitalism on the workers. In the *Grundrisse*, in particular, he admits the possibility of a drastic reduction in the working day and almost says that a greatly increased standard of living for society as a whole is a precondition for a successful revolution.

Obviously Marx's views in *Capital* on the tendency of the rate of profit to fall and the decline in working-class living standards implied a series of crises ahead for the capitalist system. Marx never produced a unified theory of the nature of these crises. It was inherent in the concept of surplus-value that the workers would produce values that exceeded the reimbursement of their labour. In the *Theories of Surplus Value*, Marx wrote:

> The greatest part of the producers, the workers, can only consume an equivalent for their product so long as they produce more than this equivalent – surplus value or surplus product. They must always be over-producers, must always produce over and above their needs, in order to be able to be consumers or buyers within the limits of their needs.

This contradiction inevitably engendered an economic crisis in which the equilibrium between sale and purchase was more or less re-established. In *Capital* Marx explicitly pointed to under-consumption as a cause of crisis:

> The last real cause of all crises always remains the poverty and restricted consumption of the masses as compared to the tendency of capitalist production to develop the productive forces in such a way that only the absolute power of consumption of the entire society would be their limit.

It was certainly Marx's general view that capitalism was an unstable system which only solved the problems it generated by creating even greater obstacles to its future progress. And the eventual conclusion was described in a famous passage at the end of Volume One of *Capital*:

Along with the constantly diminishing number of the magnates of capital, who usurp and monopolize all advantages of this process of transformation, grows the mass of misery, oppression, slavery, degradation, exploitation; but with this too grows the revolt of the working class, a class always increasing in numbers, and disciplined, united, organized by the very mechanism of the process of capitalist production itself. The monopoly of capital becomes a fetter upon the mode of production, which has sprung up and flourished along with, and under it. Centralization of the means of production and socialization of labour at last reach a point where they become incompatible with their capitalist integument. This integument is burst asunder. The knell of capitalist private property sounds. The expropriators are expropriated.

Just *when* the integument would burst asunder, Marx naturally declined to predict with any precision. Indeed, in such writings as the *Grundrisse* the impression was given that it would take a very long time for capital to exhaust all the possibilities for the extraction of surplus value from the economy. Marx anticipated, in this connection, an era of automation and a stage in capitalism in which manual labour had been replaced by machines wherever possible — an awesome prospect.

Although Marx looked forward to the inevitable collapse of the capitalist system, he was far from having a totally negative view of it. In his outline of the materialist conception of history, he wrote: 'new higher relations of production never appear before the material conditions of their existence have matured in the womb of the old society'. Thus communism was implicit in capitalism. Among the achievements of capitalism were an enormous increase in social wealth, the progressive unification of the world under a single economic system, and the creating of the possibility of an individual 'whose relationships and capacities are of a general and universal nature'. Marx even conceived of capitalism as being forced to overcome the crucial problem of the division of labour:

Modern Industry, on the other hand, through its catastrophes imposes the necessity of recognizing, as a fundamental law of production, variation of work, consequently fitness of the labourer for varied work, consequently the greatest possible development of his varied aptitudes. It becomes a question of life and death for society to adapt the mode of production to the normal functioning of this law. Modern Industry, indeed, compels society, under penalty of death, to replace the detail-worker of today, crippled by life-long repetition of one and the same trivial operation, and thus reduced to the mere fragment of a man, by the fully developed individual, fit for a variety of labours, ready to face any change of production, and to whom the different social functions he performs, are but so many modes of giving free scope to his own natural and acquired powers.

Marx considered, too, that certain of the economic forms of capitalism prepared the way for communism. He talked, for example, of share capital 'the most perfect form of capital leading to communism' and referred to the joint stock company as 'the transcendance of the capitalist mode of production within the capitalist mode of production'. There was thus a striking contrast between the increasingly social character of the capitalist process of production and the anti-social character of capitalist private property – a contrast which in itself summed up Marx's basic critique of capitalism.

It should be remembered that Marx's economics is not a unified system. He changed his mind on a number of points during the 1850s – particularly the substitution of labour-power for labour and the introduction of surplus-value which altered his perspective considerably. Thus there was a difference in approach between the rather simplistic views of capitalist breakdown in *The Communist Manifesto* and the views expressed in the *Grundrisse* which took into account the fact that the idea of 'subsistence' had a historical element in it, that parts of the working class had become better off, and that there had been a growth in social groups living on the surplus from productive labour. There is also the fact that Marx's work remained unfinished. He was always mentioning in his correspondence new materials that needed to be assimilated before he could interpret them in a scientific synthesis. Whether he was also discouraged by the sheer theoretical difficulties entailed by his own premises is an open question.

What, finally, are we to make of Marx's claim to have founded a 'science' of economics? Most importantly, science for Marx was not equated with natural science. (The German term *Wissenschaft* has a much wider connotation than the English word 'science'.) Throughout his life Marx was clear that natural science would have to lose what he called its 'one-sidedly materialist orientation' in order to be integrated in a total interpretation of man and society. Particularly in his later writings Marx emphasized that any science had to penetrate from the apparent movement of things to their real underlying causes. This involved a distinction between appearance and essence going back a long way from Hegel through Spinoza to Aristotle. Marx was distinctive in conceiving of economics as the core of any scientific view of society and in criticizing, from his early writings onwards, the current conception of economics which dealt only with the market system (appearance) without considering the social foundation (essence) in which the market was based. There are two factors which militate against treating Marx's views as scientific in the vulgar sense of theories that can be shown to be true or false by observation. Firstly, there is obviously some sort of continuity between Marx's early and later writings: the notions of alienation, man as a self-creating being, and history as a progress leading to an unalienated society are central to all Marx's work. Thus his writings always incorporate a normative element which means that they are not subject to direct refutation simply by reference to 'fact'. Secondly, Marx's economic theories are models, more or less removed from empirical reality, and they merely describe tendencies. Thus the labour theory of value is not something which is right or wrong. For Marx, it is true by definition, and the real question is whether it is able to account for the movement of prices and profits. This is a very complex question. For example, it was Marx's view that in general commodities tended to exchange at prices which were proportionate to the value embodied in them – although there might be temporary variations. In Volume Three of *Capital* Marx changed his view somewhat by admitting that what determined the exchange of commodities was much more their cost of production. And the exact relationship of values to prices has been a constant source of debate ever since. Again, central to Marx's view of the fate of capitalism was the doctrine of the falling rate of profit. Yet it is extremely difficult to determine the validity of this doctrine. In the United States, for example, profits seem on the whole not to have fallen over the last century or so – in spite of the fact that constant capital has grown much faster than the labour force. But, of course, the productivity per worker has also vastly increased and so there is no reason why profits should have declined. The most that can be said is that it is very difficult to determine the status of theories that involve so many variables.

Whatever importance he ascribed to the long-term determining effect of the economy, and however much time he devoted to analysing its present and future course, Marx was always more than an economist. He was always concerned to link his economic studies – the 'objective' side of his dialectic – with its 'subjective' side, involving the concepts of class, party and revolution through which men became politically conscious of the tensions in the capitalist economy and 'shortened the birth-pangs' of communism.

Politics

The central institution of capitalist society and the main target of Marx's politics was the state. In his early writings Marx had been concerned to emphasize the gap between civil society and the state viewed as the projection of the alienated essence of man. Later, he evolved a different (though not incompatible) view of the state as an instrument of class domination. This view is most clearly expressed in the *Communist Manifesto*:

> Political power, properly so called, is merely the organized power of one class for oppressing another . . . The executive of the modern state is but a committee for managing the affairs of the whole bourgeoisie.

Marx traced the origin of the state, together with other social institutions and classes, to the division of labour: the state was opposed to the real interests of all members of society since it constituted an illusory sense of community serving as a screen for the real struggles waged by classes against each other. In the course of history each method of production gave rise to a typical political organization furthering the interests of the dominant class. The large-scale industry and universal competition of modern capitalism had created their own political organization – the modern liberal democratic state under which the bourgeoisie could best develop their class potential.

It has already been noted that Marx's materialist conception of history was a very flexible tool of analysis – and his view of the state was no exception. Marx once said that the only perfect example of the state as an instrument of class domination was North America. For the political sphere was not merely the plaything of economic undercurrents. Sometimes, Marx said, the same economic system could give rise to different political systems. Indeed, in certain circumstances, politics could dominate economics: it was the Tudor governments, for example, that created the conditions for the existence of British capitalism; and Marx always recognized that, although England was more advanced than France economically, the political consciousness of the French was superior to that of the English.

Marx admitted two general exceptions to his characterization of the state as an instrument of class domination. The first was not gone into in great detail by Marx: in the Asian societies of India, China and, to some extent, Russia Marx saw a despotism which, being mainly based on the absence of private property in land, did not serve the interests of a particular class. The second exception was rather more important: Marx believed that in a situation where two or more contending classes were of more or less equal strength, the state could attain a large degree of independence and become a virtual parasite on the whole of society. This particularly applied to the period of absolute monarchy following the decline of feudalism. 'Modern historical research,' he wrote,

> has shown how modern absolute monarchy appeared in the period of transition when the old feudal classes were decaying and the mediaeval burgher class was evolving into the modern bourgeois class, without either of the disputing parties being able to settle accounts with the other.

And he found a more contemporary example in the French Second Empire under Louis Bonaparte.

On whatever base it was constituted, the state was, for Marx, central to the alienating structure of capitalist society, and only a revolution could displace its pervasive influence. Because the existence of the state was bound up

with the existence of classes, the state could not be
abolished piecemeal. All previous revolutions had simply
replaced one form of state by another more suited to the
changing mode of production. And the form of state that
went along with capitalism – liberal democracy – was no
exception. For although liberal democracy held that it
was open to everyone to emancipate himself by becoming
a bourgeois, by definition not everyone could do so, and
the inevitable result was the exploitation of one group in
society by another. However, the most important charac-
teristic of the next revolution – the proletarian one – was
that it would be social and not merely political: it would
not proclaim abstract rights that only a few could enjoy
but achieve a general emancipation by penetrating to the
real life of man – his socio-economic life.

Marx was no prophet and he did not go in for detailed
predictions about the future revolution. But he did say
something about when he thought there might be a
revolution, where it would break out, whether it would be
violent or not, and who would carry it out.

When? Marx was always scathing about those he
referred to as 'the alchemists of revolution' who tried to
provoke revolt whatever the socio-economic circumstances.
Not surprisingly, however, his optimism about the immin-
ence of the revolution was strongest during the two
periods when he was actively engaged in politics: the
upheavals of 1848 and the First International. In the
Communist Manifesto he declared that 'the bourgeois
revolution in Germany will be but the prelude to an
immediately following proletarian revolution'. He main-
tained this view even after the failure of the revolutionary
movement, and it was not until he resumed his economic
studies in London in 1850 that he realized that 'a new
revolution is possible only in consequence of a new crisis'
and told the workers that 'you have to endure and go
through 15, 20, 50 years of civil war in order to change

the circumstances, in order to make yourselves fit for power'. Marx's revolutionary optimism had a brief renaissance during and immediately after the Paris Commune, when he conceived of the possibility of a successful proletarian revolution in countries where the majority of the population were peasants. But his mature economic writings took a more long-term view of the economic causes of revolution and in the *Grundrisse* the impression was given that capitalism had a very long way to go before it exhausted its capacities to exploit the enormous possibilities created by machinery.

Where? The simple view of class polarization and immiserization contained in the *Communist Manifesto* seemed to imply that a proletarian revolution was uniquely a consequence of industrialization. However, between 1848 and the founding of the First International, Marx's views underwent an important change in this respect: firstly, he came to believe that workers could hope for substantial gains within the capitalist state – hence the importance he attributed to the Ten Hours Act; secondly, he realized that there was considerable differentiation within the industrial working class with the emergence of a labour aristocracy. He also came to see that potential European revolutions would be more and more contingent on the general world situation. In 1859 he referred to the opening up of California, Australia and the Far East, and continued:

Revolution is imminent on the Continent and also will immediately assume a socialist character. Can it avoid being crushed in this small corner, because bourgeois society is in the ascendant over much larger areas of the earth?

Later still, Marx began to think that Russia might prove the starting point of the revolution which 'begins this time in the East, hitherto the invulnerable bulwark and reinforcement of the counter-revolution'. And a year before his death he wrote:

> If the Russian revolution becomes the signal for a proletarian revolution in the West, so that both complete each other, then the present Russian system of community ownership of land could serve as the starting point for a communist development.

As his hopes of Russia rose, so those of Britain declined. He considered in general that the English lacked 'the spirit of generalization and revolutionary fervour'. Moreover the British proletariat as a whole had done too well out of their world economic dominance and the labour aristocracy had improved their relative standard of living too much not to dampen down their revolutionary impetus.

How? Marx did not believe in the inevitability of violent revolution. In some of the most advanced countries he considered that revolution could be introduced by peaceful means. In 1872 he mentioned Great Britain, the United States and possibly Holland in this context; and in 1880 he wrote:

> My party considers an English revolution not *necessary* but – according to historic precedents – *possible*. If the unavoidable evolution turns into a revolution, it would not only be the fault of the ruling classes, but also of the working class. Every pacific concession of the former has been wrung from them by 'pressure from without'. Their action kept pace with that pressure and if the latter has more and more weakened, it is only because the English working class know not how to wield their power and use their liberties, both of which they possess legally.

But Marx did not turn into a tame parliamentarian in his old age. He was vigorous in condemning the commune for observing too many legal niceties in a crisis situation, and not being willing to start a civil war. He declared to a conference of the International in 1871:

> We must make clear to the governments: we know that you are the armed power that is directed against the

proletariat; we will proceed against you by peaceful means where that is possible and with arms when it is necessary.

But however much Marx thought that sometimes force could be the midwife of revolution he never (except briefly in 1848 and under Tsarist conditions in Russia) approved of the use of revolutionary terror. He strongly criticized the use of terror by Jacobins in the French Revolution; its use was for him a sign of the weakness and immaturity of that revolution which had to impose by violence what was not yet inherent in society. For any revolution, if the socio-economic circumstances were not appropriate, inevitably led to a reign of terror during which the revolutionary powers attempted to reorganize society from above. Finally, Marx considered that a successful revolution – at least in the long run – was impossible if confined to one country. Marx criticized the leaders of the French proletariat in 1848 for thinking that 'they would be able to consummate a proletarian revolution within the national walls of France, side by side with the remaining bourgeois nations.' But, equally, Marx considered a strong national unity to be essential for the degree of working-class organization to produce a revolution and was strongly in favour of the unification of Germany and Italy and the resurgence of Polish nationalism.

Who? Although Marx believed that a political party was necessary to carry out a successful revolution, he never founded a party. He was only a member of any party organization for a few years and always based his political activities on existing working-class organizations. Of course, the concept of a political party in a modern sense is consequent on mass democracy and was only developing very gradually during Marx's lifetime. In the *Communist Manifesto* Marx outlined the three defining characteristics of the Communist Party as follows:

In the national struggles of the proletarians of the

M – C

different countries they point out and bring to the front the common interests of the entire proletariat, independent of all nationality. 2. In the various stages of development which the struggle of the working class against the bourgeoisie has to pass through, they always and everywhere represent the interests of the movement as a whole . . . 3. Theoretically, they have over the great mass of the proletariat the advantage of clearly understanding the line of march, the conditions and the ultimate general results of the proletarian movement.

But even the Communist League (in which Marx was active from 1847 to 1852) was never a political party in this sense: it had only about 300 members and was forced to operate in a semi-clandestine manner. Indeed, it was temporarily dissolved by Marx in 1848, and it was only in the last months of the revolution that he realized the need for a separate organized workers' party. The First International, on the other hand, was in no way a Communist Party, nor did Marx's followers form a separate group inside it. On the whole, Marx was in favour of open, democratic organization, with decisions taken by majority votes at national conferences; and he was always more willing to look for areas of agreement than of difference. Thus Marx's concept of the party was never some ideal institution, but always based on the level of organization and consciousness already in existence. Nevertheless, he did insist that this party should have a completely democratic internal organization; that it should be the independent creation of the workers themselves; that it was distinguished by a theoretical understanding of working-class goals; and that (usually) its organization was not to be a part of, or dependent on, any other political party.

There has been much debate about the kind of society a proletarian revolution would inaugurate and some criticism of the vagueness of Marx's sketches of it. But it is essential to remember that — on Marx's own principles —

any detailed predictions were bound to be baseless. For all ideas were rooted in the socio-economic soil of their time and descriptions of the future would thus be rootless ideas without any foundation in reality. Marx would have agreed completely with Hegel that 'it is just as silly to suppose that any philosophy goes beyond its contemporary world, as that an individual can jump beyond his time'. Nevertheless it is plain that for Marx the most fundamental achievement of a proletarian revolution would be (in broad terms) the changed relationship of man to nature and to his fellow-men; and, in consequence, the disappearance of political oppression in the form of the state.

For the materialist conception of history, the organization of man's productive forces was fundamental, and the proletarian revolution would be the first revolution to introduce a non-antagonistic mode of production. There would be no more occasion for the exploitation of the majority by the minority since the means of production would be in the hands of the working class, and the wealth of society would be used for the benefit of society as a whole. In particular the division of labour (which Marx believed to be at the root of so many social evils) would be abolished. In a well-known passage in *The German Ideology*, Marx stated:

> In communist society, where nobody has one exclusive sphere of activity but each can become accomplished in any branch he wishes, society regulates the general production and thus makes it possible for me to do one thing today and another tomorrow, to hunt in the morning, fish in the afternoon, rear cattle in the evening, criticize after dinner, just as I have a mind, without ever becoming hunter, fisherman, shepherd or critic. This fixation of social activity, this consolidation of what we ourselves produce into an objective power above us, growing out of our control, thwarting our expectations, bringing to naught our calculations, is one of the chief

factors in historical development up till now.

Of course, there are obvious difficulties in applying this essentially rural description to a highly developed society. In the *Grundrisse* Marx implied that the whole problem of the division of labour would be by-passed by the introduction of automated machinery and the drastic reduction in the working day: the problem then would no longer be labour but how to use leisure time. But as he grew older, he grew less sanguine: at the very end of *Capital* Volume Three he admitted that however much labour could be humanized under socialism,

> it nevertheless still remains a realm of necessity. Beyond it begins that development of human energy which is an end in itself, the true realm of freedom, which, however, can only blossom forth with this realm of necessity as its basis. The shortening of the working day is its basic prerequisite.

The resolution of problems such as the exact distribution of the social product, the role of money, and the future of marriage and the family would ultimately be dependent on the modification of human drives by changing the socio-economic basis of society. Here Marx distinguished between constant desires 'which exist under all circumstances, only their form and direction being changed by different social circumstances', and relative desires 'which owe their origin merely to a particular form of society, to particular conditions of production and exchange'. In a communist society, the former would merely be changed and given the opportunity to develop normally, whereas the latter would be destroyed by being deprived of the conditions of their existence. Marx continued:

> which desires would be merely altered under a communist organization and which would be dissolved, can only be decided in a practical way, through the changing of real, practical desires, and not through historical comparisons with earlier historical circumstances.

He went on to mention several desires (among them the desire to eat) as examples of fixed desires, and continued:

> neither do the communists envisage abolishing the fixity of desires and needs . . . they only aim to organize production and exchange in such a way as to make possible the normal satisfaction of all desires, that is, a satisfaction limited only by the desires themselves.

The political corollary of the abolition of the division of labour in communist society was the disappearance of the state. Marx stated forthrightly:

> As soon as the goal of the proletarian movement, the abolition of classes, shall have been reached, the power of the state, whose function is to keep the great majority of producers beneath the yoke of a small minority of exploiters, will disappear and governmental functions will be transformed into simple administrative functions.

What this meant in concrete terms was that communism would no longer need the typical components of the state – bureaucracy, a standing army and a professional judicature. Marx's most revealing comments in this connection are his remarks on the Paris Commune. Although Marx did not approve of all the Commune's policies, he welcomed the Commune's proposals to have all officials, including judges, elected by universal suffrage and revocable at any time; to pay officials the same wages as workmen; to replace the standing army by the armed people; and to divest the police and clergy of their political influence. Marx also believed that, given time, the initiative of the Commune could have given rise, in the country as a whole, to a decentralized, federal political structure and an economy based on co-operatives united by a common plan.

Marx was clear, of course, that a situation in which 'the normal satisfaction of all desires' was possible could not be arrived at immediately. After a successful proletarian revolution there would be a period of transition which he occasionally referred to as 'the dictatorship of the proletariat'. (It should be noted that the word 'dictatorship' did not have the same connotation for Marx as it does nowadays. He associated it principally with the Roman office of *dictatura* where all power was legally concentrated in the hands of a single man during a limited period in a time of crisis.) Even with the abolition of the division of labour and the consequent disappearance of the state, communist society would still 'in every respect, economically, morally and intellectually, be stamped with the birthmarks of the old society from whose womb it emerges'. Only after a considerable period could full communism be attained. This communism Marx described in a famous passage which can serve as an apt summary of his ultimate goal:

> In a higher phase of communist society, after the enslaving subordination of the individual to the division of labour, and therewith also the antithesis between mental and physical labour, has vanished; after labour has become not only a means of life but life's prime want; after the productive forces have also increased with the all-round development of the individual, and all the springs of co-operative wealth flow more abundantly – only then can the narrow horizon of bourgeois right be crossed in its entirety and society inscribe on its banners: From each according to his ability, to each according to his need!

The aim of this concluding chapter is to give a historical sketch of the different interpretations to which Marx's thought has been subject. This is necessary for an understanding of Marx because his ideas have been overlaid by a series of reinterpretations, some of which are highly misleading. However impossible it may be to uncover some essentially 'real' Marx, an appreciation of Marx's ideas is easier once these interpretations have been placed in historical and political perspective.

Three main reasons can be distinguished for the capacity of Marx to seem all things to all men. Firstly, many of his doctrines really *were* ambiguous. In his youth, Marx had detected an ambivalence in his master Hegel; and the same ambivalence was present – not surprisingly – in the disciple. For they were both dialectical thinkers and the Marxian dialectic in particular was open-ended: being a unity of subjective and objective factors, both the theory and the practice were constantly interacting and evolving. Marx had not offered any hard and fast conclusions – only a methodology. This ambivalence was heightened by the fact that Marx's work was unfinished: of his vast projected 'Economics' only the first volume of the first part – Volume One of *Capital* – was ever completed. In addition, Marx's power for sustained creative work deserted him during the last illness-ridden decade of his life. So he was not able to contribute to the debate that began after the Paris Commune and the publication of *Capital*; and it was only in the 1880s that his doctrines gained widespread attention. Marx's views on some of the subsequent applications of his theory can be gauged from his comment on certain French

'Marxists': 'As for me, I am *not* a Marxist!'

The second reason for the changing nature of what came to be known as Marxism was its becoming the doctrine of a mass movement. Mass political parties were born in the second half of the nineteenth century and socialism was the most radical, appealing to all who were excluded from, or not getting enough of, the benefits of the new industrial society. What distinguished Marxism in this context was its rare ability to link revolutionary fervour and desire for change with a historical perspective and a claim to be scientific. Almost inevitably, the ideas were simplified, rigidified, ossified. Marxism became a matter of simple faith for its millions of adherents to whom it gave the certainty of final victory. But this entailed its transformation into a dogmatic ideology with the correlative concept of heresy – or revisionism as it was often called. (The parallels with certain periods in the history of the Christian religion are obvious.) Only a very selective version of the sacred texts could be propagated and if, even then, history did not conform – then history itself had to be re-written.

The third factor was the chaotic state in which Marx left his manuscripts at his death. For not only was his work unfinished: he had also left rough drafts that went beyond what he had actually published and – at least in the mind of many – implied a thorough reassessment of Marx's message. The publication of Marx's early writings around 1930 and the *Grundrisse* in 1941 are the most striking examples.

It is an important fact (given excessive prominence in the orthodox Communist interpretation of Marx) that Marx had had a lifelong friend and collaborator in Friedrich Engels. Not only did Engels constantly give Marx moral and financial support: he also had a considerable influence on Marx's thought. It was Engels in 1844 who guided Marx's interest to economics and introduced him at first hand to British capitalism; Marx relied on him, too, for advice on military and scientific matters. But the fact that Engels survived Marx by thirteen years enabled him to have an even greater impact on the interpretation of Marx's thought just as it was beginning to become the official doctrine of a mass political movement. Engels was the keeper of Marx's archives and the authoritative exponent of Marx's ideas – beginning with his editing Marx's manuscripts for the remaining volumes of *Capital*. He was a quick and lucid writer, a vulgarizer in the best sense possible, and the systematization and clarity of his works gave them a much wider circulation than any of Marx's writings. Engels's contribution was to assimilate Marx's views more and more to the prevailing positivism and scientism – a process begun with Engels's speech at Marx's graveside: 'Just as Darwin discovered the law of development of organic nature, so Marx discovered the law of development of human history.' This assimilation received its most popular exposition in *Anti-Dühring*, which for decades after Marx's death continued to be accepted as the classical account of the Marxist *Weltanschauung*. In his attack on the socialist philosopher Dühring, Engels proclaimed the Marxian dialectic to be 'the science of the general laws of motion and development of nature, human society, and thought'. More specifically, the most important of these laws were the law of the transformation of quantity into quality, of the interpretation of opposites, and of the negation of the negation. (Of course, Marx also called his doctrines 'scientific' (see Chapter 3 above), but the term had much less the connotation of natural scientific methodology in his work – after all, even Hegel had called his work 'scientific'.) These laws were thought by Engels to be operative in a nature that was objectively given and independent of the human mind. Thus the world of nature and the world of human history were two separate fields of study – whereas for Marx one of the central aspects of his dialectic had consisted precisely in the interaction of man and his surroundings – a view stemming from Hegel. Engels did indeed claim to be simply applying Hegel's dialectic, and, in a sense, Hegel also saw a dialectic in nature but it was still subject to the universal mediation of human consciousness. The concept of matter as some kind of *materia prima* is entirely foreign to Marx (see Chapter 3 above).

During the two decades after Engels's death, Marx's ideas came to dominate the socialist movement in Western Europe and, in particular, its largest and best organized party, the German Social Democratic Party. For the orthodox Marxists of the SPD, led by Karl Kautsky, Marx was primarily a great economist who had demonstrated with scientific rigour the inevitable collapse of capitalism and the victory of the proletariat. This view was already under attack by the Revisionist school. Their chief protagonist was Edward Bernstein who had been much influenced by the Fabian socialism he had met in England. Bernstein considered himself a Marxist but thought that Marx needed revising to fit his ideas to the world of modern industrial democracy. He denied that classes were polarizing and their struggle sharpening, and advocated a socialism that would be introduced peacefully by reform rather than revolution. This view was sharply contested by Kautsky who, as the champion of Marx's ideas against heresy, carried further and into new fields the systematization begun by Engels. He emphasized those aspects of Marx's work which laid stress on the determination of history by economic causes, and preached a value-free, scientific Marxism in which history was governed by immutable laws. In the Revisionist controversy, Kautsky could plausibly claim to be the upholder of orthodoxy, but it should be remembered that Marx's ideas were chiefly

74

known through the stark proclamations of the *Communist Manifesto* or the difficult volumes of *Capital*: less than half of what Marx had written – including work that was to throw a different light on many of those debates – had so far been published. Kautsky and the leaders of the loose federation of Marxist parties known as the Second International most evidently departed from Marx's ideas in the ever-growing gulf between their theory and their practice. For however much they might protest their orthodoxy in such matters as the class struggle and the inevitability of socialism, their practice had to be adapted to the needs of an established party with an increasingly bureaucratic structure operating in a democracy. Inevitably it was more concerned with pulling in votes and conserving its established status and organization than with promoting revolutionary efforts that ran the risk of destroying all its hard-won achievements – an ambiguous situation much like that in which the French and Italian Communist Parties currently find themselves.

The German Social Democrat current of Marxism was shattered by the outbreak of the First World War. Having become so involved in the political structure of their country, they found it impossible to resist the tide of patriotic fervour and voted for the war credits. The abortive revolution of 1918 and the rise of Fascism meant the eclipse of Marxism in Germany for many decades. The centre of revolutionary dynamism moved eastwards – as Marx had begun to suspect might be the case towards the end of his life. The Marxism that eventually triumphed in Russia owed a great deal to indigenous elements. In the famous dispute between Mensheviks and Bolsheviks two of the main issues were whether Russia was on the eve of a bourgeois revolution with the proletarian one a long way off, and how centralized the revolutionary party should be. These were both problems that bothered Marx during the 1848 upheavals – not surprisingly, for that was the period when German conditions most resembled the semi-feudal, semi-capitalist Russia of the first two decades of this century. Marx's writings of this period could provide some support for Lenin's curious idea of a proletariat leading a 'bourgeois' revolution, his positive attitude to the peasantry as an essential component of the revolution, and even the idea of permanent revolution that Lenin adopted from Trotsky in April 1917. On the whole, however, the Mensheviks' idea that the revolution could not be hastened and their distrust of a highly centralized party structure were more in accord with Marx's general views. Thus it is not surprising that the Bolsheviks put more emphasis on the political side of Marx's writings than did the German Social Democrats: it is recorded that Lenin knew Marx's circulars to the Communist League 'by heart' and 'used to delight in quoting them'. But the Leninist theory of the party went far beyond anything that Marx had suggested. For Lenin believed that the working class could not by itself achieve a revolutionary consciousness which needed to be instilled in them by a 'vanguard' party. He, therefore, wished to see the whole working-class movement subject to a small, highly disciplined and highly centralized party of professional revolutionaries, most of whom were class-less intellectuals.

After the success of the 1917 revolution the ever-growing power of Stalin entailed the formulation of Communist doctrine as a state ideology as far removed from Marx as were the decisions of the Council of Trent from the New Testament. Marx himself had had something to say about a premature revolution having to resort to terror to maintain itself in power, and the idea of a vanguard party soon led to the proletariat's finding itself expropriated by an increasingly dictatorial party machine and eventually by a single man. The monolithic view of the world as subject to dialectical laws which was prominent in Engel's *Anti-Dühring*, and which Lenin continued, reached its apogee in the Stalinist textbooks on dialectical materialism – a phrase first used by Lenin's mentor Plekhanov. The working class were merely the passive recipients, whether of doctrines or of five-year plans, that had been worked out 'above'. The one major innovation of Stalin in Marxist doctrine and the main source of his quarrel with Trotsky was the idea of 'socialism in one country' – a view with which Marx would have been distinctly out of sympathy.

In the face of such a rigidification of Marxist theory, a reaction was inevitable. The diminishing vitality of Marxism as a theory went hand in hand with a decreasing interest in the Hegelian elements present in Marx culminating, during the Stalinist period, with the condemnation of Hegel as a reactionary thinker pure and simple. It is significant that Lenin himself just before the 1917 revolution had begun to appreciate the significance of Hegel for Marx. But it was George Lukács who rediscovered in full Marx's debt to Hegel and expounded Marx's whole thought, including his economics, within the framework of a social humanism. He restored to the interpretation of Marx the centrality of the notion of alienation – a concept that had been almost entirely absent from Engels onwards. Lukács in his seminal *History and Class Consciousness* (1923) re-introduced the vision of alienated man transcending his alienation through proletarian class consciousness and revolution. As an Hegelian, Lukács rejected the tendency of previous decades to reduce Marxism to a factual science. To suppose that existing social arrangements were governed by the kind of immutable laws operative in physical science was, for Lucács, to suffer an illusion. In this illusion social reality took on the 'objective' appearance of something external and independent of men, 'reified' as Lukács called it, instead of being seen as the creation of man. Social facts could only be given meaning by understanding the structure of the totality. This totality was dynamic and its highest point yet reached was in the class consciousness of the proletariat (viewed as an 'ideal type' of Lukács's teacher Weber), which provided the vantage point for viewing current social reality. And in the ultimate analysis this higher class consciousness was identical with Marxism itself. It is a startling fact that Lukács's interpretation of Marx was written *before* the publication of Marx's early writings which contained much that supported his views. Nevertheless Lukács's ideas did not get wide publicity at the time, although writers like Korsch and Gramsci stressed the need for Marxists to engage in intellectual debate and criticized the mechanistic themes of the Marxism of the Second International.

For many interpreters of Marx's thought, the publication of the early writings around 1930 marked a decisive turning-point. (The impact came later in the English-speaking world – the first translation of the EPM was not published until 1959.) These writings – and particularly the EPM – revealed a Marx very different from either the rather arid economist of Kautsky or the dialectical materialist of Soviet dogma. Marx appeared to be a philosopher, a humanist with not only a devastating account of the alienation of man in capitalist society but also a rich and varied account of the potential latent in every individual waiting to be realized under communism. The subsequent enthusiasm for the early Marx was helped by two factors: first there had been a revival of interest in Hegel of which the work of Lukács was but one symptom. And since the early writings of Marx were those that most directly showed the influence of Hegel, the ground was well prepared. Secondly, there was a political factor: the leading Marxist theoreticians had previously been at pains to claim that their *Weltanschauung* was totally different from that of the bourgeoisie. However, in order to combat the menace of Fascism, Marxists in general were much more willing to admit the similarities between Marx's humanism and the humanism of the liberal bourgeoisie as against the barbarities of Nazi and Fascist ideology viewed as a rejection of the western European traditions.

The stifling of intellectual life in Germany during the 1930s and the Second World War meant that – at least in the Western world – serious attention only came to be paid to Marx's early writings in the late 1940s. The widespread enthusiasm for existentialist doctrines at this time ensured a welcome reception for the 'young' Marx. Typical was the wide-selling book by Erich Fromm, *Marx's Concept of Man*, in which Marx was hailed as a spiritualist existentialist and comparisons were made between Marxism and Zen Buddhism. Christian-Marxist dialogue became common: after all, both Kierkegaard and Marx could be viewed as sharing an existential revolt against Hegel. In the calm and prosperous 1950s it was difficult sometimes to believe in the increasing pauperization of the proletariat and the necessity of its coming to a realization of its revolutionary role. The growing manipulative power and anonymity of technology, on the other hand, caused many radicals to take up Marx's account of the alienation of man in capitalist society and claim that, in this connection, Marx's views were more relevant the more wealthy and complex society became. The subjective factor in man's picture of his world was being increasingly emphasized, whether in psycho-analysis or with the stress in linguistics on the active role of language in shaping human knowledge. And Marx, too, came to be acceptable to many as a thinker aiding man's self-comprehension by means, for example, of his doctrine of ideology.

In Eastern Europe where Marxism, instead of being the creed of the underdog, had been enthroned as the ruling ideology, there was obviously room to point out that the communist man of the EPM did not have much to do with state bureaucracies of the Stalinist type, and the cautious thesis was advanced, by writers such as Adam Schaff, that alienation could exist even under socialism. Study of the early writings was seen by many anti-Stalinist Marxists as a return to the original source of communist thought, much as the Reformers used the New Testament to show up abuses rife in the later mediaeval Church. Up to the present time this process has had little effect: Bloch and Kolakowski have left their countries, Garaudy has been expelled from the French Communist Party, and the Praxis group of Jugoslav philosophers is increasingly isolated.

With the publication of Marx's early works, the interpretation of his thought came increasingly to concentrate on the question of its continuity: were there two Marxes – an early and a late – or only one? The old Stalinist interpretation dismissed the early writings as so many *juvenilia* rendered quite superfluous by his later works. And others who wished to minimize the importance of the early writing stressed the infrequency with which Marx later used terms such as 'species-being' and 'alienation' that were so central to the EPM. Quite the contrary view was taken by the first editors of the German edition of the rediscovered writings. For them, the EPM was 'the cardinal point of Marx's whole life's work' which 'sets out in its complex web of philosophical, economic and historical discussions the unity and totality of Marx's intellectual contribution'. The even later publication of the *Grundrisse* showed both extreme positions to be mistaken, but the precise nature of the 'continuity' is still the subject of much controversy.

In recent years in the western world two main currents of Marxian interpretation have achieved prominence. The first is that of the Frankfurt School of 'critical' theorists such as Adorno, Habermas and Marcuse. The critical theorists aim to restore the philosophical dimension to Marxism and, retaining an enviable confidence in the power of human rationality, have developed a series of concepts intended to go beyond Marx to interpret the changes that have taken place in the world since his death. These consist mainly in adding the dimension of social psychology to Marx's work and emphasizing the basic proposition that, if society is increasingly under the artificial control of technocrats, then any purely empirical approach to social reality must end up as a defence of that control. The most striking statement in this context is Habermas's *Knowledge and Human Interests*. The influence of Freud – so manifestly absent from previous Marxist writing – has been felt by the whole Frankfurt School but in particular by Herbert Marcuse whose *Eros and Civilization* attempted a synthesis of Freud and Marx. But it was *One Dimensional Man* which made Marcuse famous, particularly when some of its ideas seemed to offer an interpretation of the student revolts of the late 1960s. Marcuse's pessimism about the revolutionary potential of a proletariat dominated (along with the rest of society) by an all-pervasive technocratic ideology led him to place his faith in the substratum of the outcast and outsiders, the exploited and persecuted minorities such as students and blacks which would involve a meeting of 'the most advanced consciousness of humanity and its most exploited force'. Obviously there is no direct parallel in Marx to the students, and the appeal to a force *outside* society is more reminiscent of the anarchists than of Marx, whose views on the *Lumpenproletariat* were the exact opposite.

The second current interpretation – the school of Althusser – is worth spending a little more time on in that it represents itself as a direct interpretation of Marx. Taking advantage of the current prestige of structuralist linguistics, psychology and anthropology, it is the aim of Althusser to 'rehabilitate' Marx as a structuralist before his time. Thus Althusser continues the Stalinist division of an early pre-Marxist Marx and a later scientific Marx – though with a conceptual sophistication quite foreign to the previous versions of this view. Roughly speaking, structuralism is the view that the key to the understanding of a social system is the structural relationship of its parts – the way these parts are related together by the regulative principle of the system. And Althusser's search for a timeless rationality reminiscent of Comte (for whom Marx himself had no time) involves the banishment of both history and philosophy. When applied to Marx this involves cutting his work into two separate conceptual structures with the dividing point around 1845. Any reading of Marx as a humanist, a Hegelian or a historicist must (since these ideas are clearly contained in his early works) be rejected. Since it has become increasingly implausible to claim (particularly after the publication of the *Grundrisse*) that there are no humanist or Hegelian elements in the later Marx, a 'real' Marx has been uncovered employing a methodology – never clearly defined – almost totally at variance with concepts that he actually employs.

In spite of their being so clearly at variance in many places with what Marx actually *said*, the ideas of Althusser have had considerable success. For Althusser's Marx is clearly incompatible with existentialism and radical versions of Christianity and thus attractive to those who felt that their commitment was becoming diluted by 'dialogue'. Its esoteric emphasis on theoretical analysis and disdain for empirical work is also welcome to intellectuals. Obviously anyone is entitled to revise Marx – but it is disingenuous to claim that such revisions really represent a return to Marx.

Finally, what of the paradox that Marx, a Victorian thinker who saw Europe and North America as the centre of the world stage and the arena for future revolutions, is apparently now more widely respected as a *mentor* by the populations of Third World countries? Marx himself cerainly emphasized the European limitations of his theory of historical development. He talked of the Asiatic mode of production, but did not integrate it into his scheme of historical development. According to him this mode of production was static and destined to be overtaken by the spread of capitalism over the whole globe. Thus Marx was is ambivalent on colonialism as he was on capitalism – both were destructive and inhuman but at the same time regenerative in that they laid the foundations for a new form of society. This emerges particularly from Marx's analysis of the British in India. There is little in African socialism or Chinese communism that represents a distinct interpretation of Marx himself. It is most important to bear in mind in this connection that Marx envisaged a communist revolution taking place in countries where a certain degree of economic well-being would permit considerable post-revolutionary political freedom. In the event, however, Marxist doctrines have proved most successful in those countries where scarcity of resources mean that political freedom is a luxury they cannot afford. In many developing countries a version of Marxism combined with nationalism functions as an ideology for mass participation in the modernization process. The central doctrines of Maoism, the 'mass line' and the encirclement of the towns by the countryside – which spring mainly from the experience of extended guerilla warfare – are far removed from the original ideas of Marx, though obviously in the broad scheme of Marxism the people of Asia, Africa and Latin America can be substituted as an 'external proletariat' in the place of the industrial working class in which Marx placed such hope, and the theory of imperialism can take the place of Marx's exploitation.

The ideas of Marx – revised, distorted, rediscovered – have been the inspiration of a large section of humanity over the last hundred years. The history of their influence

has shown the validity of the conclusion of Ignazio Silon
with which, I think, Marx himself would not have dis
agreed:

> The more Socialist theories claim to be 'scientific', th
> more transitory they are; but Socialist values are per
> manent. The distinction between theories and values i
> not sufficiently recognized, but it is fundamental. On
> group of theories one can found a school; but on a group
> of values one can found a culture, a civilization, a new
> way of living together among men.

How to Read Marx

nyone setting out to read Marx in English is faced with problem : there is an embarrassingly large collection of lected writings of one sort and another, yet no complete orks. The latter started publication, in London and New ork, early in 1975 and will be appearing regularly over e next dozen years or so – finally to total a daunting ty volumes. Meanwhile, the Foreign Languages Publishing ouse in Moscow has produced separate editions of many Marx's works. Although the introductions and notes are ten written from an extremely committed point of view, e translations themselves are quite faithful.

Undoubtedly the best short piece of Marx to read is the *ommunist Manifesto*. Although Marx realized it needed dating (see the Preface to the Second German Edition) was continually willing for it to be re-edited and transted as a summary of his views. There is a cheap Penguin ition (though the long introduction is unfairly hostile to arx) and even cheaper editions from Moscow and Peking.

The next work to read is the first part of *The German eology* (the last two-thirds consists largely of turgid lemic) which contains Marx's longest discussion of storical materialism – rich and exciting reading. There is paperback edition of the relevant portion published by wrence and Wishart in 1970.

With the *Communist Manifesto* and *The German Ideology* hind him, the reader can branch out in a number of rections. He should on no account miss Marx's analyses current events in such brilliant pieces of polemical jourlism as *The Eighteenth Brumaire of Louis Bonaparte* and *e Civil War in France* (both in the Moscow *Selected*

Works). Marxian economics can be rather difficult and
good introduction is provided either by *Wage-Labour a.
Capital* written in 1848 or the 1865 *Value, Price and Pro
(also both contained in the *Selected Works*). The latter is
summary of the main ideas of *Capital* and, since it w
a lecture delivered to British Trade Unionists of who
intellectual capacity Marx had a very low opinion, it is
simple as possible. *Capital* Volume One itself is by :
means as difficult as is sometimes believed. The fi
250 pages or so deal with rather abstract (but perfec
intelligible) economic concepts, but the second half co
tains analyses of Victorian capitalism which show not on
Marx's historical method at work but also how great
literary talent he possessed. Volume Two is rather techni
and only for the really keen; Volume Three, edited fr
the manuscripts, has none of the polish of Volume O
but contains important material – particularly the l.
section on the Trinitarian formula.

For an appreciation of the genesis of *Capital* and its pla
in Marx's work as a whole, a reading of the *Grundrisse*
vital. It gives a fascinating picture of Marx at work. But
is also the most difficult of Marx's writings. For those w
wish to tackle the whole 800 pages there is a Peng
edition with a perceptive introduction; for the l
ambitious, Paladin have a much shorter selection conta
ing the most important passages.

No understanding of Marx is complete without so
knowledge of the early writings. The most important a
the *Economic and Philosophical Manuscripts* (translated
full in the Milligan and Bottomore editions). The parti
larly interesting sections are 'alienated labour', 'priv
property and communism', and 'critique of Hegel's d
lectic' which should be read in that order and at least twi
(These three sections are also translated in the Easton a
Guddat and McLellan editions.)

The best short edition of selected writings is that

ottomore and Rubel. The 'classical' selection is the
Moscow *Selected Works* which has the advantage of mainly
reproducing pieces whole, though there are no early writings and the commentary is sometimes rather tendentious.
Most of the others suffer from being largely selections from
the Moscow selections and not including more recent new
material. With this proviso, the two best are those edited
by Tucker and by Bender. The forthcoming selection by
McLellan is intended to be as widely representative as
possible.

Now to the necessarily rather more subjective question
of commentaries. The present writer almost inevitably
thinks that the best simple introduction to Marx's ideas is
his own *The Thought of Karl Marx: an Introduction*.
Fischer's *Marx in his own words* and Sanderson's *The
Political Ideas of Marx and Engels* are also good introductions. At a slightly more advanced level two excellent
commentaries are Avineri's *The Social and Political
Thought of Karl Marx* (which emphasizes Marx's debt to
Hegel) and Evans's *Marx* (which gives a good all-round
analytical and historical introduction). A little more difficult is Ollman's *Alienation* which offers a re-interpretation
of Marx's thought in terms of that concept.

Turning to more specialized fields, two good books introducing Marx's sociology are: Zeitlin's *Marxism: An Introduction* and Lefebvre's *The Sociology of Marx*. For Marx's
politics, a book with a wealth of detail and accurate
interpretation is Hunt's *The Political Ideas of Marx and
Engels*. The best way to appreciate Marx's approach to
history is to read some of its practitioners – Hill, Hobsbawm and Thompson, for example – though a good
account is to be found in Fleischer's *Marxism and History*.
Marx's economics are definitely not easy, but probably the
best introduction is Mandel's short *Introduction to Marxist
Economic Theory* followed by the same author's *The
Formation of the Economic Thought of Karl Marx*. Those

who want something rather more technical could tr
Desai's *Introduction to Marxian Economics*.

An area where a commentary of some sort is almos
essential is Marx's early writings: the books by Dupr
McLellan and Howard all cover the ground with as muc
clarity and concision as possible. Kamenka's *The Ethic*
Foundations of Marxism has a slightly more philosophica
approach; Maguire's *Marx's Paris writings* is the mos
extensive commentary available on the work of 1844; an
Tucker's *Philosophy and Myth in Karl Marx* is a provoca
tive and influential account of Marx as a pseudo-religiou
thinker.

Those interested in the orthodox communist interpreta
tion of Marx can read Garaudy's *Karl Marx: The Evolutio*
of his Thought or Lewis's *The Life and Teaching* (
Karl Marx. The 'classical' critique of Marx's historica
materialism can be found in Acton or Plamenatz. As fo
biographies there are two excellent short ones by Berli
and by Blumenberg; Mehring had provided the standar
full-length one for decades; and now – hopefully – McLella
is the most comprehensive and reliable. This last als
contains a fuller bibliography than space here permits.

Chronology

1818   Birth of Marx

1835   Study at University of Bonn

1836   Study at University of Berlin

1837   *Letter to his Father*

1841   Submits Doctoral Thesis

1842   Articles for *Rheinische Zeitung*

1843   Marries Jenny von Westphalen; moves to Paris; *Critique of Hegel's Philosophy of Right; The Jewish Question*

1844   Editor of *Deutsch-französische Jahrbücher; Economic and Philosophical Manuscripts* (EPM)

1845   Moves to Belgium; *Theses on Feuerbach*

1846   *German Ideology*

1847   Joins Communist League

1848   *Communist Manifesto*. Moves to Germany to edit *Neue Rheinische Zeitung*

1849   *Wage-Labour and Capital*. Moves to London

1850   *The Class Struggles in France*

1852–62   Articles for *New York Daily Tribune*. *The Eighteenth Brumaire of Louis Bonaparte*

1856   Moves to Grafton Terrace

1857/8   *Grundrisse*

1859   *Critique of Political Economy*

1862/3   *Theories of Surplus Value*

1863   Death of Mother

1864   Moves to Maitland Park; Foundation of First International; *Inaugural Address*

1865   *Value, Price and Profit*; drafted *Capital* Vol. 3

1867   *Capital* Vol. 1

1869   Engels moves to London

1871   The Paris Commune; *The Civil War in France*

1875   *Critique of Gotha Programme*

1881   Death of Jenny Marx

1882   Preface to Second Russian Edition of *Communist Manifesto*

1883   Death of Marx

Select Bibliography

A Multi-Volume Collections

K. Marx, F. Engels, *Works*, Lawrence and Wishart, London, International Publishers, New York, 1975 ff.

K. Marx, *The 1848 Revolutions, Surveys from Exile, The First International and After*, ed. D. Fernbach, Penguin, London; Monthly Review, New York, 1973 ff.

K. Marx, *On Revolution, On Press Freedom and Censorship*, ed. S. Padover, McGraw-Hill, New York, 1971 ff.

B Single-Volume Collections

K. Marx, F. Engels, *Selected Works*, Moscow, 1935
(several reprints)

K. Marx, *Selected Writings in Sociology and Social Philosophy*, ed. T. Bottomore and M. Rubel, Watts, London, 1956

Marx–Engels, *Reader*, ed. R. Tucker, Norton, New York, 1971

K. Marx, *The Essential Writings*, ed. R. Bender, Harper and Row, New York, 1972

K. Marx, *Selected Writings*, ed. D. McLellan, Oxford University Press, 1975

Writings of the Young Marx on Philosophy and Society, ed. L. Easton and K. Guddat, Doubleday, New York, 1967

K. Marx, *The Early Texts*, ed. D. McLellan, Blackwell, Oxford; Barnes and Noble, New York, 1971

C Single Works

K. Marx, F. Engels, *The Communist Manifesto*, ed. A. J. P. Taylor, Penguin, London, 1967

K. Marx, F. Engels, *The German Ideology*, Part One, ed. C. Arthur, Lawrence and Wishart, London; International Publishers, New York, 1970

K. Marx, *Grundrisse*, ed. M. Nicolaus, Penguin, London; Monthly Review, New York, 1973

K. Marx,	*Marx's Grundrisse*, ed. D. McLellan, Paladin, London; Harper Torchbook, New York, 1973
	Capital, translated S. Moore and E. Aveling, London, 1887. Many subsequent re-editions.

D   *Commentaries*

H. B. Acton,	*The Illusion of the Epoch*, London and New York, 1955
L. Althusser,	*For Marx*, New York and London, 1970
S. Avineri,	*The Social and Political Thought of Karl Marx*, Cambridge University Press, 1968
I. Berlin,	*Karl Marx, His Life and Environment*, Oxford University Press, 1939
W. Blumenberg,	*Karl Marx*, New York and London, 1971
L. Dupré,	*The Philosophical Foundation of Marxism*, New York, 1966
M. Evans,	*Marx*, London, 1975
E. Fischer,	*Marx in his own words*, New York and London, 1970
R. Garaudy,	*Karl Marx. The Evolution of his Thought*, New York and London, 1967
J. Habermas,	*Knowledge and Human Interests*, Heinemann, London, 1972
D. Howard,	*The Development of the Marxian Dialectic*, Carbondale, 1972
R. Hunt,	*The Political Ideas of Marx and Engels*, Pittsburgh University Press, 1974
E. Kamenka,	*The Ethical Foundations of Marxism*, New York and London, 1962
H. Lefebvre,	*The Sociology of Marx*, New York and London, 1968
J. Lewis,	*The Life and Teaching of Karl Marx*, New York and London, 1965
G. Lukács,	*History and Class Consciousness*, New York and London, 1971
E. Mandel,	*An Introduction to Marxist Economic Theory*, New York, 1971
E. Mandel,	*The Formation of Marx's Economic Thought*, New York and London, 1971
D. McLellan,	*Marx before Marxism*, New York and London, 1970
D. McLellan,	*The Thought of Karl Marx*, New York and London, 1971

D. McLellan,   *Karl Marx. His Life and Thought*, New York and London, 1973

J. Maguire,   *Marx's Paris Writings*, Dublin, 1972

H. Marcuse,   *One-Dimensional Man*, Boston, 1964

H. Marcuse,   *Eros and Civilization*, New York, 1967

F. Mehring,   *Karl Marx*, London and New York, 1936

B. Ollman,   *Alienation: Marx's Critique of Man in Capitalist Society*, Cambridge University Press, 1971

J. Plamenatz,   *German Marxism and Russian Communism*, London and New York, 1954

J. Sanderson,   *An Interpretation of the Political Ideas of Marx and Engels*, London and New York, 1969

R. Tucker,   *Philosophy and Myth in Karl Marx*, Cambridge University Press, 1961

I. Zeitlin,   *Marxism: A Re-examination*, New York, 1967

The Fontana Economic History of Europe

To be completed in six volumes, each book is made up of individual sections written by a leading European or American specialist. For the convenience of students each section is published separately in pamphlet form as soon as possible, the volumes appearing when all the contributions have been received.

The general editor of the series is Carlo M. Cipolla, Professor of Economic History at the Universities of Pavia and California, Berkeley.

'There can be no doubt that these volumes make an extremely significant addition to the literature of European economic history, where the need for new large comparative works has long been felt . . . It is overall a project of vision and enormous value.'

Times Literary Supplement

Already published

1. The Middle Ages

Contributors: Cipolla: J. C. Russell: Jacques Le Goff: Richard Roehl: Lynn White Jr.: Georges Duby: Sylvia Thrupp: Jacques Bernard: Edward Miller.

2. The Sixteenth and Seventeenth Centuries

Contributors: Cipolla: Roger Mols: Walter Minchinton: Hermann Kellenbenz: Aldo de Maddalena: Domenico Sella: Kristof Glamann: Geoffrey Parker.

3. The Industrial Revolution

Contributors: André Armengaud: Walter Minchinton: Samuel Lilley: Gertrand Gille: Barry Supple: R. M. Hartwell: J. F. Bergier: Paul Bairoch: Donald Winch: M. J. T. Lewis.

4. The Emergence of Industrial Societies

Part 1: Contributors: Claude Fohlen: Knut Borchardt: Phyllis Deane: N. T. Gross: Luciano Cafagna: Jan Dhondt & Marinette Bruwier.
Part 2: Contributors: Lennart Jörberg: Gregory Crossman: Jordi Nadal: B. M. Biucchi: William Woodruff: B. R. Mitchell.

In preparation

5. The Twentieth Century

6. Contemporary Economics

Fontana Politics

Battle for the Environment Tony Aldous

The English Constitution Walter Bagehot
Edited by R. H. S. Crossman

Tocqueville Hugh Brogan

The Backroom Boys Noam Chomsky

For Reasons of State Noam Chomsky

Problems of Knowledge and Freedom Noam Chomsky

Selected Writings of Mahatma Gandhi
Edited by Ronald Duncan

Marx and Engels: Basic Writings
Edited by Lewis S. Feuer

Governing Britain A. H. Hanson and Malcolm Walles

The Commons in Transition *Edited by* A. H. Hanson and
Bernard Crick

Europe Tomorrow *Edited by* Richard Mayne

Machiavelli: Selections *Edited by* John Plamenatz

The Cabinet Patrick Gordon Walker

The Downfall of the Liberal Party 1914-1935
Trevor Wilson

The Conservative Party from Peel to Churchill
Robert Blake

Fontana History

Fontana History includes the well-known History of Europe, edited by J. H. Plumb and the Fontana Economic History of Europe, edited by Carlo Cipolla. Other books available include:

Fontana Social Science

Books available include:

African Genesis Robert Ardrey

The Territorial Imperative Robert Ardrey

The Social Contract Robert Ardrey

Racial Minorities Michael Banton

Ideology in Social Science
Edited by Robin Blackburn

The Sociology of Modern Britain
Edited by Eric Butterworth and David Weir

Social Problems of Modern Britain
Edited by Eric Butterworth and David Weir

Men and Work in Modern Britain
Edited by David Weir

Strikes Richard Hyman

The Dominant Man H. Knipe and G. Maclay

Strike at Pilkingtons Tony Lane and Kenneth Roberts

Figuring Out Society Ronald Meek

Drugs, Science and Society Alan Norton

Dockers David Wilson